The Use of Biodiversity in International Law

This book presents a legal genealogy of biodiversity – of its strategic use before and after the adoption of the Convention on Biological Diversity, 1992.

This history of 'genetic gold' details how, with the aid of international law, the idea of biodiversity has been instrumentalized towards political and economic aims. A study of the strategic utility of biodiversity, rather than the utility of its protection under international law, the book's focus is not, therefore, on the sustainable or non-sustainable use of biodiversity as a natural resource, but rather on its historical use as an intellectual resource. Although biodiversity is still not being effectively conserved, nor sustainably used, the Convention on Biological Diversity and its parent regime persists, now after several decades of operation. This book provides the comprehensive answer to the question of the convention's continued existence.

Drawing from environmental history, the philosophy of science, political economy and development studies, this book will be of interest to advanced undergraduate and postgraduate students in Environmental Law, International Law, Environmental Studies, and Ecology.

Andreas Kotsakis is a Senior Lecturer in Law at Oxford Brookes University, UK.

Part of the Law, Science and Society series

Series editors
John Paterson, *University of Aberdeen, UK*
Julian Webb, *University of Melbourne, Australia*

For information about the series and details of previous and forthcoming titles, see https://www.routledge.com/law/series/CAV16

A GlassHouse book

The Use of Biodiversity in International Law

A Genealogy of Genetic Gold

Andreas Kotsakis

a GlassHouse Book

First published 2021
by Routledge
2 Park Square, Milton Park, Abingdon, Oxon OX14 4RN

and by Routledge
52 Vanderbilt Avenue, New York, NY 10017

A GlassHouse Book

Routledge is an imprint of the Taylor & Francis Group, an informa business

© 2021 Andreas Kotsakis

The right of Andreas Kotsakis to be identified as author of this work
has been asserted by him in accordance with sections 77 and 78 of the
Copyright, Designs and Patents Act 1988.

All rights reserved. No part of this book may be reprinted or reproduced
or utilised in any form or by any electronic, mechanical, or other means,
now known or hereafter invented, including photocopying and recording,
or in any information storage or retrieval system, without permission in
writing from the publishers.

Trademark notice: Product or corporate names may be trademarks
or registered trademarks, and are used only for identification and
explanation without intent to infringe.

British Library Cataloguing-in-Publication Data
A catalogue record for this book is available from the British Library

Library of Congress Cataloging-in-Publication Data
Names: Kotsakis, Andreas, author.
Title: The use of biodiversity in international law: a genealogy of genetic
gold/Andreas Kotsakis.
Description: 1. | Milton Park, Abingdon, Oxon; New York, NY:
Routledge, 2021. | Includes bibliographical references and index.
Identifiers: LCCN 2020049686 (print) | LCCN 2020049687 (ebook) |
ISBN 9781138849099 (hardback) | ISBN 9781315725840 (ebook)
Subjects: LCSH: Environmental law, International. | Biodiversity
conservation–Law and legislation.
Classification: LCC K3585 .K675 2021 (print) | LCC K3585 (ebook) |
DDC 344.04/6–dc23
LC record available at https://lccn.loc.gov/2020049686
LC ebook record available at https://lccn.loc.gov/2020049687

ISBN: 978-1-138-84909-9 (hbk)
ISBN: 978-0-367-75240-8 (pbk)
ISBN: 978-1-315-72584-0 (ebk)

Typeset in Bembo
by Deanta Global Publishing Services, Chennai, India

Contents

Acknowledgements		vi
Introduction: Backwaters		viii
1	The 'undead' convention and environmental reason	1
2	Lambswool into synthetic: Early programmes	23
3	The glare of international law and the grand bargain	42
4	The genetic gold rush	61
5	The regulation of genetic gold	78
	Conclusion: Still here	96
	Bibliography	107
	Index	115

Acknowledgements

This book may have a single author, but it is at the same time very much a product of an institution, a culture, and lineage. It possesses its own genealogy. A number of events and decisions contributed to this final product in front of you, the reader. Doing justice to the full context of this book is impossible, but these next few words will nevertheless attempt this task.

I would like to first and foremost thank my parents, Kostas and Pelagia, for imparting a critical and inquisitive attitude and an – at times – obsessive commitment to knowledge, and for raising me in a house filled with books and discussion. It would have been impossible to reach this point without their unwavering emotional and material support through the many years and struggles of doctoral study and early academic career. I would also like to thank my partner, companion, and wife Cora Lingling Xu, who showed me a better way of living and working, and who supported me through the process of finalising this book, suffering for every chapter and page as I did.

The book is an offshoot of research conducted for my doctoral thesis many years ago. I would like to thank Veerle Heyvaert for building my confidence and expertly guiding me through the whole PhD process to the best possible conclusion, and also Martin Loughlin for the perpetual tough questioning during my time at LSE. I would also like to thank Nick Piška for endless debates at our rundown London flat, and for valiantly battling through an incomprehensible draft to offer direct and productive comments. Andreas Mihalopoulos-Philippopoulos has provided steadfast support and continuing inspiration for many years. Colin Perrin has been a calm presence at Routledge, always supportive and patient despite the delays that this book suffered. I would also like to thank the anonymous reviewers of my book proposal, as well as the book series editors, John B Patterson and Julian Webb, for their creative questions, inquisitive comments, and constructive criticism. The book has benefitted greatly from this process, but, of course, all errors and misconceptions remain my own. I would like to thank the critical legal conference crew, where parts of this book have been presented, and in particular Vito De Lucia, for research collaboration and inspiration.

Acknowledgements   vii

This book is a child of the UK's Research Excellence Framework. It was made possible by research leave granted by my institution, Oxford Brookes University, on the basis that this would constitute an 'output' to be 'returned' in this administrative exercise. I would like to thank the research leads and mentors in Oxford, Lucy Vickers and Peter Edge, for their continued support and for gently pushing the institution to commit to this research leave and the completion of the book project. Without their calm but firm encouragement, this book would not have been finished. At the Faculty of Humanities and Social Sciences, Gary Browning has for years led and fostered a research culture, working from inside an institution that appears often perplexed by the modern demands and challenges of academic scholarship. It is this culture that enabled the production of this book. I would also like to thank my LLM students at Oxford Brookes University over the years for their critical engagement and for allowing me to work through some of the ideas presented in this book.

Finally, I would like to reiterate that this book is a child of the UK's Research Excellence Framework. It has been conceived, written, or rather revised, updated, and edited in brief snatches of time, during the summer or in some exhausted 'research days' during semester time. There was never any time to develop the ideas and argument in a calm manner. Everything was pressured, frantic, agitated. It is a snapshot of thinking, not the thinking itself. The broader context of British universities has both enabled and constrained this book. Without the REF, this book may have never been finished – but also without the REF this book would never have been finished in its current form.

Oxford, 14 August 2020

Introduction
Backwaters

'Biodiversity is one thing that some people, like point zero zero zero zero zero one percent of the world's population care about'[1]

If one were to write a history of the UN Convention on Biological Diversity,[2] they could trace a genealogy, with the treaty being the key node in a line of evolution that would roughly go like this: *problem – proposal – treaty – institution*. The intrepid scientist discovers a significant problem in the natural order of the world; they develop a theory about the sources of this problem and how to address this; they begin advocating for their theory and solutions; the world finally listens and takes action; new institutions and ways of doing things are instituted; a teleological historical account that can also serve as the script for a Hollywood movie, with the requisite 'happy ending'.

The treaty would be the key turning point of this genealogical account, a sign of acceptance of the existence of the problem and the proposal for its solution, as well as a platform for further action. This is the biodiversity convention, in force for almost 30 years now. Its history can certainly be framed and presented along these lines. The treaty provides vindication of the ecological concern with the problem of generalized erosion of habitats and extinction of species of plants, animals and other organisms across the planet. It provides the basis for taking concerted, global action to address this global problem. Such an account would fit with the field of international environmental law and its self-conception of its own progressive historical role.[3] It would fit with the field's own form of internationalism; the universal story of humanity's growing realization of major environmental problems and the valiant efforts of the international community to address them, via the universal instrument of international law. This would ultimately be a story of a noble struggle, another great project for the international community and belief in humanity's capacity to perform 'good'. It would vindicate the existence of the contemporary 'global biodiversity regime' as a natural evolution of the original agreement, suggest ways to reform, improve, and move forward. This book does not present such a genealogy of the biodiversity convention.

Given the dismal state of the world's biodiversity,[4] the convention and its voluminous formal output would equally be far too easy to 'trash' anew, following the best/controversial traditions of critical legal theory.[5] One takes the protocols, recommendations, declarations, and statements of the convention seriously and then proceeds to expose their profound inconsistencies and compromises, as well as the lack of tangible effect in terms of the status of the world's biodiversity or even changing state practice. Lawyers that would never self-identify as belonging to that particular school of legal thought have already presented such work, dismissing the biodiversity convention outright.[6] The disjunction between grand principles and non-existent obligations, between grand strategic goals and absence of any material means to achieve them, the embrace of soft law coupled with the absence of any normative effect permeates the whole edifice of the convention. The only aspect that seemed to be missing was a toxic institutional culture, replete with misconduct and discrimination – and it now appears that somehow the convention acquired this as well in recent years.[7]

The convention lends itself easily to being a target of multiple questionings, in respect of both the conceptual and legal coherence of the treaty, as well as of the overall effectiveness of the resulting endeavour of a global biodiversity regime. Such a critique would have its basis on a subversive and dismissive genealogy, leading to verdicts of irrelevancy or failure. After all, it seems that international environmental law's somehow inherent progressive credentials often shield its institutions from critique. They are peculiar sacred cows, always fledgling and precious, besieged at all times; always to be reformed, never to be abandoned. Resplendent in its Nietzschean fervour, it would be called something dramatic like 'the death of biodiversity', echoing the infamous polemics on the end of environmentalism that have proliferated in recent decades.[8] This book does not present such a critical genealogy either.

But this book does present a type of genealogy of biodiversity – of a third kind; a genealogy of the use to which biodiversity has been put, conceptually and politically, over several decades and through the instrument of an international environmental agreement, of the instrumentalization of the idea of biodiversity towards certain aims, of its framing so as to achieve certain ends, with the aid of international law. The focus is not on the sustainable or non-sustainable use of biodiversity as a natural resource, but on the political use of biodiversity as a conceptual resource. It is about the utility of biodiversity, politically and legally, rather than the utility of law or politics in protecting biodiversity. A particular use of biodiversity, identified by the term 'genetic gold', is the focus. This is the proposition that biodiversity, predominantly held in the territory of the Global South, has significant economic value as 'raw' genetic resources for the biotechnology industry. The notion that biodiversity constitutes genetic gold made it a useful resource, but also altered both the ecological concern and the international agreement associated with it.

This genealogy neither vindicates, nor subverts the biodiversity convention. It does not vindicate it, because it does not discover some foundational origin that can restore the treaty's full authoritative glory. It does not subvert it, because it does not seek to throw stones at an empty husk of a legal treaty. Nor does it seek to merely document and build a historical archive of its legal discursive output. Instead, this genealogy seeks to present a type of 'mesh' that surrounds the biodiversity convention and allows it to continue to operate; to make visible a series of linkages, assemblages, struggles, conflicts, and breaks that have built the edifice of the global biodiversity regime, and to present the whole contingent composition of this regime's underlying grid of rationality, which is identified in the book with the term 'biodiversity reason'.

Why should we care about the biodiversity convention, genetic gold and biodiversity reason, these constructs of a decades-long biodiversity project, made out of disparate parts? And why examine them in this particular, genealogical, way? To answer the first question, because the complex/structure/mesh is a type of 'laboratory', where 'technologies' of government have been and continue to be developed. Genetic gold is simply one such technology. In response to the second question, because genealogy is the method, the instrument, that allows for the detection of the operation of this laboratory, guided by biodiversity reason.

The research presented therein is, therefore, a work of excavation and tracing, of bringing this laboratory of biodiversity reason to light. Picking the idea of biodiversity apart, the genealogy cannot but veer towards the idea of genetic gold that dominated the first decade of the treaty's operation, under a notional grand bargain between the Global North and South. By making a clear distinction between the genetic gold rush and its promises, the failed aftermath, and the delayed response of international environmental law in the shape of the Nagoya protocol, this work reaches its main argument that despite its failure, genetic gold contributed to a conceptual structure, a biodiversity reason, that is still in use today.

The celebrated conservation biologist Elliot Norse once likened the biodiversity movement to a rapid river, strengthened by new tributaries and flowing into a growing 'sea' of public attention.[9] But this was the 1990s, by all accounts the high point of interest, both scholarly and public, in biodiversity. There is no movement now and the sea is parched, as the opening quote acknowledges in a visceral manner. The advantage of this laboratory is thus its hidden location in the putative backwaters of international environmental law. Out of sight, out of the glare of the spotlight of climate change, and the Anthropocene scholarship and scrutiny, the machine is churning.

And as for those who insist that the biodiversity convention does not matter because of its failure to arrest the global rates of biodiversity decline, all I can ask is are you confident that was the intention?

Notes

1 Peter Kareiva, chief scientist of the Nature Conservancy, quoted in Jessica Dempsey, *Enterprising Nature: Economics, Markets, and Finance in Global Biodiversity Politics* (Wiley Blackwell 2016), 91.

2 Convention on Biological Diversity (1992), 31 ILM 818. (CBD)
3 Peter H. Sand, 'The Evolution of International Environmental Law' in Daniel Bodansky and others (eds), *The Oxford Handbook of International Environmental Law* (OUP 2007).
4 IPBES, Global assessment report on biodiversity and ecosystem services of the Intergovernmental Science-Policy Platform on Biodiversity and Ecosystem Services. E. S. Brondizio, J. Settele, S. Díaz, and H. T. Ngo (eds.). IPBES secretariat, 2019.
5 On the North American variant of critical legal studies see Mark Tushnet, 'Critical Legal Theory (without Modifiers) in the United States' (2005) 13 *The Journal of Political Philosophy* 99; Mark Tushnet, 'Some Current Controversies in Critical Legal Studies' (2011) 12 *German Law Journal* 290. On the British variant see Matt Stone and others (eds), *New Critical Legal Thinking: Law and the Political* (Routledge 2012); Costas Douzinas and Adam Geary, *Critical Jurisprudence: The Political Philosophy of Justice* (Hart Publishing 2005). On 'trashing' as method specifically see Mark G. Kelman, 'Trashing' (1984) 36 *Stanford Law Review* 293.
6 Stuart R. Harrop and Diana J. Pritchard, 'A Hard Instrument Goes Soft: The Implications of the Convention on Biological Diversity's Current Trajectory' (2011) 21 *Global Environmental Change* 474
7 Karl Mathiesen, 'UN biodiversity chief quits. Documents show she had been accused of misconduct' *Climate Home News* (31/10/2019) at: https://www.climatechangenews.com /2019/10/31/un-biodiversity-chief-quit-key-summit-accused-misconduct/#:~:text=Ea rlier%20this%20month%2C%20Cristiana%20Pa%C8%99ca,mixture%20of%20factors %20increasingly%20affecting. Accessed: 20 July 2020.
8 Michael Schellenberger and Ted Nordhaus, *Break Through: From the Death of Environmentalism to the Politics of Possibility* (Houghton Mifflin Co 2007).
9 Elliot A. Norse, 'A River that Flows to the Sea: The Marine Biological Diversity Movement' (1996) 9 *Oceanography* 5.

Chapter 1

The 'undead' convention and environmental reason

Whatever happened to biodiversity?[1]

You see these buildings breaking apart and coming down? He looked at me. You don't think this is what we're supposed to see when we look at these buildings? He wanted nothing to do with this idea. You don't think it's a new way of seeing?[2]

This chapter argues that the standard motif to international environmental law scholarship – underpinned as it is by a progressive teleology of an active international community that aims to protect the global environment and by an ahistorical urgency to take problem-solving action now in anticipation of a looming catastrophe – is incapable of explaining the paradoxical and persistent existence of the biodiversity convention. This is a convention that has seemingly not achieved anything tangible in terms of its formally stated goals and has in fact allowed the continued decline and loss of biodiversity around the world. The chapter then discusses legal genealogy as an alternative approach, capable of uncovering in more detail the formulation of the biodiversity convention and its underlying rationality, its particular environmental reason.

A snapshot of the biodiversity convention

The biodiversity convention is a framework treaty with the aim of addressing the problem of global biodiversity loss that was concluded in May 1992 and entered into force on 29 December 1993. Two supplementary main protocols to the convention have been concluded and are now operational: the Cartagena Protocol on Biosafety,[3] which was agreed in 2000 and entered into force in 2003, and the Nagoya Protocol on Access to Genetic Resources and the Fair and Equitable Sharing of Benefits Arising from their Utilization,[4] which was agreed in 2010 and entered into force in 2014. A third agreement, the Nagoya – Kuala Lumpur Supplementary Protocol on Liability and Redress, was agreed in 2010 and entered into force in 2018.[5] Collectively, the legal texts, decisions, and plans, along with their elaborate institutional framework, are often referred to as the biodiversity (treaty) regime. A regime in this sense can be defined as 'a set of norms, rules and procedures that structure the behaviour and relations

2 The 'undead' convention

of international actors so as to reduce the uncertainties they face and facilitate the pursuit of a common goal'.[6]

The treaty defines 'biological diversity' as 'the variability among living organisms from all sources including, *inter alia*, terrestrial, marine and other aquatic ecosystems and the ecological complexes of which they are part; this includes diversity within species, between species and of ecosystems'.[7] Its thematic scope is thus exceptionally wide, encompassing all three commonly understood levels of genetic, species, and ecosystem diversity. It is a treaty concerned with all life on Earth. The convention's actual jurisdictional scope, however, is limited by the fact that according to the convention biodiversity remains a national resource, under the sovereign control of member states.[8]

There are three main treaty objectives, which are the conservation of biodiversity, the sustainable use of its components, and the fair and equitable sharing of benefits arising from the utilization of genetic resources.[9] The three objectives form the three 'pillars' of the convention's operation. Arguably, an additional overarching objective, not explicitly stated in the main text of the treaty,[10] is 'to achieve an equitable balancing of the interests of developed and developing states' in the areas of nature conservation and natural resource use.[11]

Conservation primarily refers to the designation and management of protected areas, but also extends to the general protection and management of ecosystems, habitats, and biological resources within national jurisdiction.[12] This form of *in situ* conservation, prioritized in the treaty,[13] is traditionally seen as the predominant conservation activity, a perception only heightened by continuous habitat destruction and terrestrial species decline over the decades. This remains the case today. Contemporary thinking maintains that 'protected areas are the cornerstone of biodiversity conservation'.[14] According to the Aichi targets,[15] the strategic aim was to protect and effectively manage 17% of all terrestrial and inland habitats and 10% of all marine and coastal areas globally by 2020.[16] The treaty also includes, as 'complementary measures', *ex situ* conservation of biodiversity components in research facilities and various collections.[17] Article 9 specifically addresses the establishment of new facilities and collections. Given the size of existing collections, this provision significantly reduces the impact of the convention in key areas, such as agricultural/plant biodiversity.

Sustainable use is defined as: 'the use of components of biological diversity in a way and at a rate that does not lead to the long-term decline of biological diversity, thereby maintaining its potential to meet the needs and aspirations of present and future generations'.[18] This objective introduces and makes biodiversity conservation 'subject to the greater objective of sustainable development',[19] forming a clear link between biodiversity and the principle of intergenerational equity.[20] It also dates instantly the convention as a legal document of the 1990s.

The third objective of fair and equitable benefits sharing is not explicitly defined in the treaty text itself. Based on the Nagoya Protocol, benefit sharing applies to genetic resources specifically, rather than the broader term biological resources of the first two objectives. In the legal vocabulary of the regime, these genetic resources are to be 'utilized', as opposed to 'used' (the term employed in the context of biological resources). Utilization (as opposed to use) means 'to conduct research and development on the genetic and/or biochemical composition of genetic resources'.[21] Genetic resources were essentially conceived as the resources needed for the biotechnology industry, defined as 'genetic material of actual or potential value',[22] where genetic material 'means any material of plant, animal, microbial or other origin containing functional units of heredity'.[23] This legal category of genetic resources also includes derivatives,[24] i.e., naturally occurring biochemical compounds without functional units of heredity, such as scents, colourings, and the like.

The benefits that need to be shared in this way arise from their 'utilization', i.e., the specific use of these genetic resources and applications by biotechnology.[25] What constitutes fair and equitable sharing was defined in practice by reference to a number of provisions read together,[26] including the protection of local and indigenous communities, knowledge, and lifestyles.[27] The Nagoya Protocol is understood as an instrument for the implementation of this third objective, creating a so-called access and benefit sharing (ABS) regime, based on principles of national sovereignty over genetic resources, prior informed consent and mutually agreed terms.

The expansive scope and ambitious objectives are countenanced by the limited jurisdictional scope. The convention itself is not directly charged with the conservation or management of any resources, species, or areas. There are no special provisions or annexes for endangered species or areas, an approach favoured by other nature-related conventions.[28] They did exist originally, but were subsequently removed from the draft negotiating text.[29] The treaty regime thus relies on national implementation. It provides a framework of soft commitments, based on the treaty text, and relies on national action and legislation to achieve its normative effect. In other words, it has an indirect responsibility, charged with encouraging, supporting, facilitating, and incentivising its member states to implement laws, policies, and plans that in turn encourage, support, facilitate, and incentivize action by states and non-state actors towards the fulfilment of its objectives.

Boasting an extremely wide scope, but non-existent jurisdiction, thus being completely reliant on national implementation to achieve its objectives, the convention possessed no option but to internationalize the main treaty goals of biodiversity conservation, sustainable use, and benefit sharing. The expansive scope and ambitious objectives were controversial from the outset of negotiations, especially related to the third 'pillar' of fair and equitable distribution, and the unstated fourth objective of a grand, North–South balance. Controversy and contestation, recounted in chapter 4 therein, prompted the use of broad and vague language throughout the treaty text, with all commitments being additionally tempered with many qualifications, such as 'as far as possible' or

4 The 'undead' convention

'as appropriate'. Without this linguistic approach, leading to the dilution of normative effect and the increase in flexibility, the treaty would not have been concluded.[30]

The primary commitment that a state signing up to this treaty regime (and all the word's states bar the US have done so) assumes is the development or adaptation of 'national strategies, plans and programmes' (and rather pointedly legislation is not part of this short list) for the conservation and sustainable use of biodiversity, using the indicative lists of relevant measures included in the convention as a basis.[31] These plans have the eloquent acronym of NBSAPs (National Biodiversity Strategies and Action Plans) in the convention's nomenclature. These NBSAPs are conceived as policy instruments. A second concrete and unconditional commitment is to submit national reports to the conference of parties on implementation and progress towards the convention's objectives.[32] Beyond these two obligations, every other commitment is heavily qualified.

Spectres of treaty death

The first specialized study of international environmental agreements was a diagram of a set of principles and obligations on the verge of becoming established as a separate sub-field of international law.[33] It was published in 1985. Its normative aspirations, its desire to establish the field's identity are clear. This diagram also contained a stark image of the death that awaits all defective environmental treaties, in the analysis of the *de facto* defunct Western Hemisphere Convention,[34] as 'a sleeping convention'. A sleeping convention was empty legal text with no real-world effect, attributed by the author to its lack of institutional machinery (in the shape of regular conference of the parties and the like) capable of applying and maintaining any form of pressure for compliance, implementation, or even attention by member states.[35] The Western Hemisphere Convention was still a binding legal treaty, ostensibly creating legal obligations for its signatories, but had become an irrelevant and unused instrument. The image – and fear – of this 'eternal sleep' was thus emblazoned onto the consciousness of the field.

The lesson from the tale of the sleeping convention was swiftly learned. If the problem was their deficient institutional practices, then environmental treaties would be outfitted (or retrofitted) with elaborate institutional and administrative structures (including conferences of the parties, secretariats, standing scientific bodies and working groups, amongst others) to counteract the threat of irrelevancy. This transformed them into dynamic and elaborate *treaty regimes*. The latter were thus seen as a solution, averting the spectre of death. Environmental treaties had to spawn regimes in order to survive.

The spectre of the sleeping convention certainly influenced the institutional structure of the CBD. In addition to standard treaty organs, such as a governing body in the shape of a regular conference of the parties,[36] a secretariat,[37] and the scientific body, clearing house mechanism, and financial mechanism discussed earlier, a number of subsidiary bodies and working groups, established by the COP, have complemented the operation. This includes a Subsidiary Body on Implementation,[38] which began work in 2016, and a scientific body, the Subsidiary Body on Scientific, Technical and Technological Advice.[39] There are *seven* thematic work programmes,[40] as well as dozens of work programmes on cross-cutting issues.[41] Equivalent structures have also been adopted for the two main protocols to the convention, and the meetings have started to be held concurrently to reduce the costs of participation, particularly for representatives from Global South states.[42] COP meetings are attended by the UN specialized agencies, the IAEA,[43] as well as non-party states,[44] and any other agencies and bodies, including NGOs, can be observers.[45] This is an active, lively, dynamic convention.

Dynamism, progress, belief, and indeed hope were hallmarks of early international environmental law. In the 1990s one could indeed still claim that 'the provisions in the new agreements are generally more stringent and detailed than in the previous ones, the range of subject matter broader, and the provisions for implementation and adjustment more sophisticated'.[46] Excitement about the future was in the air, when an esteemed international law professor would welcome the advent of a 'new world order' uncritically and unironically, and international environmental law represented a new way of international law-making.[47] Lessons that Simon Lyster first proposed were now seemingly being learned at an accelerated pace by states willing to cooperate at the international level. There was an expectation for more agreements, initiatives, and actions, designed in a more competent and coherent manner. During that era, the biodiversity convention was able to capitalize and deliver on this front, adding a protocol and expanding its institutional machinery.

The sun has now set on this era of progress in international environmental law. Different spectres swiftly emerged, suggestions of 'treaty congestion',[48] 'ossification',[49] and 'dissonance',[50] of a field swiftly reaching 'infirm old age'[51] before its time. To counteract such dismissals, there was the view that the 2000s were simply a period of 'retrenchment and consolidation', whereby the switch from rule and principle creation to the issue of effectiveness was a sign of 'maturation'.[52]

Despite this gloom in academic analyses of the field, the biodiversity convention seemed to be bucking the trend. Impressively outfitted with elaborate institutional machinery developed over two decades and centrally ensconced as a key node within the wider global biodiversity regime comprised of several multilateral biodiversity-related agreements, 2010 was the year it was supposed to be celebrating. The UN had declared the International Year of Biodiversity, in order to bring renewed global attention and awareness to the problem of biodiversity loss.[53] The 10th Conference of the Parties was held at Nagoya in October of that year and produced two significant outcomes: the aforementioned Nagoya Protocol, a belated international legal response to the genetic

6 The 'undead' convention

gold rush that occurred during the 1990s, and a new strategic plan for the convention for the period 2011–2020, including a set of detailed biodiversity targets (the 'Aichi targets').[54]

This impressive outcome was the culmination of discussions and negotiations (eight years in the case of the protocol) undertaken within a dynamic regime that contained a sprawling collection of mechanisms, working groups, institutions, partnerships, boasting near-universal membership by all states (there are 196 parties to the convention). By adopting the best organizational practices that international environmental law had deemed as necessary, it was able to present to the world the image of an evolving and functioning regime, while the gears of the climate change convention were grinding down. A direct comparison with the difficulties and rancour of the equivalent conference of the parties of the 'other' Rio Convention at Copenhagen in the preceding year, greatly favoured the spirit and effectiveness of the biodiversity convention. The optics were excellent. 2010 was supposed to be a successful, if not triumphant, year. Buoyed by enthusiasm over these achievements, towards the end of 2010 the UN declared the forthcoming 2011–2020 decade as the United Nations Decade on Biodiversity, to further promote the implementation of the convention's objectives, Aichi targets, and strategic plan that spanned the same period.[55]

Yet if one looked carefully, the thin veneer of triumphant success was easy to peel away; it was all bluster and cheap façade. The Nagoya conference was billed in the world's media as a global biodiversity 'summit', with the usual high-level ministerial segment boasting participation by heads of state. Yet ultimately the conference was attended by the heads of state from Gabon, Guinea-Bissau, Yemen, Monaco, and Japan (being the host), while a significant number of states did not send any ministerial-level representation, following what had become a long-term trend of state practice vis-à-vis the convention. This was evidence that biodiversity no longer commanded a significant place or attention in the increasingly congested global agenda. On second glance, the optics were actually not that good, and self-aggrandising 'UN-speak' that 'a new era of living in harmony with Nature (sic) is born'[56] or the direct historical comparisons with Kyoto made by the Executive Secretary of the CBD[57] were rather fanciful, if not the wrong note to hit outright. It made the subsequent billing of the Nagoya outcome as a loosely termed 'global deal on nature' tenuous at best. It was, in the words of George Monbiot, a 'ghost agreement' that was not really a substantial agreement.[58] Although it now appears that every new step of the CBD will be given a similar billing as a global deal – as is the case for the third strategic plan currently being formulated. This appears to be one lesson on overpromising still not learned.

The thin veneer not only extended to secondary issues of diplomatic prestige, field status, or global attention, but also to demonstrating an actual positive effect in terms of biodiversity itself. This was, in fact, the second strategic plan adopted, after the first one had failed to meet its goal. In 2002, nine years after its entry into force, the convention's operation had been organized for the first time through a strategic plan with the primary objective of achieving, by 2010, 'a significant reduction of the current rate of biodiversity loss at the global, regional and national level as a contribution to poverty alleviation and to the benefit of all life on earth'.[59] The CBD were responding to the problems identified with implementation and compliance with the adoption of a strategic target. This plan and target were well-received at the ensuing World Summit of Sustainable Development at Johannesburg in 2002 and incorporated into the existing Millennium Development Goals (MDGs).[60]

Yet the Nagoya Conference could only acknowledge[61] the dismal finding of the third edition of the *Global Biodiversity Outlook* that the 2010 target of this first strategic plan had not been met, and that most indicators pointed towards the continuing decline of genes, species, and ecosystems diversity.[62] There remained, therefore, a lack of direct, meaningful impact in terms of arresting the decline of biodiversity across the world, a rather central element of the whole project. We now also know that the second strategic plan has also failed in meeting the Aichi Biodiversity Targets at its conclusion in 2020.[63] Despite its best efforts, therefore, and two strategic plans, the biodiversity convention has for the past decade at least been experiencing its own brush with the old spectre of the 'sleeping convention', albeit in a modified, modern form. It had followed the recipe, yet the food did not come out as promised.

These cracks in the façade can rather easily be contrasted with the celebratory and aspirational tone of the convention, which seemed, in 2010, to be doubling down on a bet to maintain the illusion of progress. In addition to the Nagoya protocol,[64] a new – second – strategic plan proposed a grand vision of a future 'living in harmony with nature', with the even grander goal, 'where by 2050, biodiversity is valued, conserved, restored, and wisely used, maintaining ecosystem services, sustaining a healthy planet and delivering benefits essential for all people'.[65] The strategic plan was not accompanied by any concrete form of national implementation mechanism other than the pre-existing obligation for states to submit National Biodiversity Strategy and Action Plans, a treaty regime practice that dates back to the primary treaty text in 1992. This vision of a harmonious relation still drives the convention to the present day; it drives the current discussions and negotiations for the post-2020 biodiversity framework,[66] i.e., the third strategic plan that the convention is preparing to adopt. A new 'inspirational and motivating 2030 mission' and 'a coherent, comprehensive and innovative communication strategy' are on the cards for that plan, as an intermediate step on the road to fulfilling the 2050 vision of living in harmony with nature.[67]

And therein lies a peculiar phenomenon, consisting of a combination of absent global interest, declining status within the international community, law and policy failure, with a seemingly unaffected, continuous, streamlined production of consistent institutional output, in the form of decisions, agreements, policies, strategies, and plans. A peculiar phenomenon, where the gulf

8 The 'undead' convention

between the importance and expression of self-imposed goals and the lack of means, instruments, and institutions to achieve them has only ever grown wider. Certainly not a sleeping convention by any means, but is there any effect to its stream of utterances? Maybe to avoid sleep, it has been awake for too long. It is, in its own particular way as one of the celebrated Rio conventions of 1992, 'too big to fail'.

The paradox of the 'undead convention'

The biodiversity convention has reached the crossroads of a paradox. The convention forges ahead, while biodiversity loss also continues apace. Let the regime grow, and biodiversity decline. Let new plans be agreed, and old targets remain unfulfilled. Decades of operation have resulted in reorientations of approach and additional protocols, building complexity without a concomitant increase in authority. The one salient characteristic of this regime is that it *persists*. In the face of criticism, failure, and irrelevancy, it continues to operate. A strange new spectre can be perceived; a new type of 'sleeping convention' no longer abandoned due to lack of correct institutional practices, but a regime that shuffles on insouciantly despite the presence of such practices, producing a lot in terms of output and little in terms of global purpose or impact. The convention is not allowed to 'die', yet cannot 'live'. An *undead* convention prowls the field of international environmental law.

How can we explain this paradox? The available tools of critical legal analysis appear insufficient. For example, we can talk about the difference between 'law in the books' and law on the ground/in practice. This approach manifests when we discuss the gap between the universal scope claimed by the convention and its absolute reliance on national implementation. We can discuss the gap between aspirational scope and real jurisdiction. We can easily deduce that the treaty regime has been hampered and hamstrung since the very beginning of the agreed text of the treaty. Lamenting the increasingly soft law nature of the convention implies that 'hard', binding law is or may be a solution to its problems. None of these approaches helps us specifically explain the continued existence and persistent, albeit seemingly vacuous, operation of this treaty regime. None of these approaches focuses specifically on the gap between the consistent legal and policy output and the continued biodiversity decline around the world, on the character of the undead convention shuffling on.

This is because these approaches do not go beyond the standard motif of international legal enquiry in the area of the environment, and that motif is an obstacle to our understanding of the paradox. This motif is based on a particular – and fixed – relation to both science[68] and history;[69] namely, this motif is about maintaining distance from both.

In relation to the former, there is an acceptance of a form of ecological truth of biodiversity loss. The nature, aspects, and elements – the formulation – of the environmental problem itself is of no interest. The focus is on the response to the problem, what international environmental law can seemingly provide. The overall sentiment is that, as lawyers, 'we start from the premise that such a threat exists, even though the exact magnitude, the underlying causes of biodiversity loss, and the nature of its impact, may be subject to debate'.[70]

It is easy to observe this motif in action. The legal inquiry starts with the weight of scientific facts on the current extinction crisis. In order to impress the gravity of the problem of biodiversity loss upon its audience, it will have to resort to some scientific facts and metrics: total number of species, rates of extinction and ecosystem degradation, acres of endangered habitats and protected areas, and the like should be paraded for the purpose of establishing urgency. This is then counterposed with the positive image of biodiversity as the web of life and Earth's life support system, providing essential resources and services. Often the declining Amazon rainforest, as the eternal symbol of biodiversity, receives a lament. Any reputable report or scientific study will do as a source for these numbers and figures, the more recent the better; as long the juxtaposition between decline and wonder is stark, and the alarm is raised.

This initial litany has a dual role, both methodological and substantive. It establishes the ecological context of the legal inquiry, as well as the scientific evidence base for biodiversity as a problem requiring urgent action at the international level. It grounds and frames the legal analysis, which functions under the shadow of perpetual, ahistorical, urgent environmental crisis. The inquiry will analyze and develop definitions, principles, rules, and institutions in response to the notional 'brief' it has received from ecology regarding biodiversity loss and the required action. A normative 'this, then, needs to be done' in terms of remedies and institutional creation or reform will then conclude the successful inquiry.

Legal scholarship's response to an externally defined premise of an environmental problem of biodiversity loss will have been delivered. But this common premise is not to be revisited as part of the legal inquiry. It is, after all, external to law itself and the core of a legal inquiry. The problem, in this case the decline of global biodiversity, can never be questioned as an outcome of any legal inquiry into the biodiversity convention and the global regime that has emerged around it. The environmental problem becomes a closed scientific *a priori*, on which to build normative proposals for reform and remedies. Scientific closure begets legal closure.[71]

Consequently, this form of inquiry has nothing to offer regarding the paradox of elaborate normative production, in the shape of new institutions, principles, and rules, based on sound biodiversity knowledge, but yet with no appreciable impact or effect. If both the problem of biodiversity loss and the biodiversity convention constitute separate disciplinary containers, walled-off from each other, no comprehensive view is possible.

In relation to history, the motif reflects an inherent belief in the historical unveiling of progressive reason in the shape of decisive and effective international action to protect the environment (and in the case at hand conserve biodiversity). The fixed, linear history of the evolution of any international legal instrument follows in three acts. In the first act, the origin: intrepid scientists discover the problem of biodiversity decline, struggle to be heard, but eventually bring this problem to global attention; the international community acts to address the problem through the means of an international, multilateral treaty. In the second act, obstacles emerge with this treaty, states, and corporations often in the way. Disagreements and interests abound; now the intrepid lawyers must work to modify the approach and overcome these. The crisis intensifies, and there is an urgent need to act to address the problem. The odds are not in their favour. In the third and final act, in the final hour, disagreements are overcome, and consensus is reached; a global deal is signed. Crisis is averted at the last instance, and a new dawn of the international community working together can be celebrated. This motif is prevalent because of environmental law scholarship's unacknowledged relation with history and overall lack of historical awareness.

This is a soothing historical narrative that serves the self-imagination of the field of international environmental law as humanity's representative in the heroic encounter with environmental problems. This teleology of progression from ignorance of the environmental problem to universal action, and in the continuous evolution of general principles of international law towards more environmental – or at least sustainable – ends cannot but support the contemporary biodiversity convention as the pinnacle of its evolution. This teleology eternally repeats and mimics the evolution of the field of environmental law itself. It is the continuous playing out of its Rachel Carson's blueprint, on a global stage. A legal-scientific sermon for our troubled times; first, a warning from ecology, then law comes in, before the solution is presented, in the third act. It is always a matter of additions, tweaks, incremental reforms, keeping things going, more binding obligations on states, different decision-making structures, or, in recent years, the addition of economics. International environmental law can only ever do good, and it only needs a small helping hand to realize its lofty, aspirational goals. The broader inability to move beyond a fixed conception of international legal history exposes history as the international environmental law's significant blind spot. It is a field that cannot countenance history, except in very linear narrow terms as legal history – a succession of legal events, decisions, and texts, in response to external problems and processes.

It is, therefore, this standard motif of legal inquiry that has created this paradox. The reality is so far from the model, that the model itself needs to be revisited. The field behaves as if we are basking in the glow of this third and final act, which contradicts the reality of continuing biodiversity loss and the historical lack of impact. Consequently, to understand this paradox, the biodiversity convention needs to be exposed to different kinds of analyses, using different kinds of sources. The motif needs to be set aside, which requires rethinking the relation of the field with science and history.

It is submitted here that the documents produced by the treaty regime should not constitute the primary sources for such analyses. Dating back to 1994 and the first conference of the parties of the biodiversity convention, there are 25 years of meetings and decisions for a legal scholar to analyze; a voluminous formal discourse on global biodiversity and its decline is, of course, available. A focus on such sources would reinforce the disciplinary closure of the standard motif. Nor are so-called secondary legal sources useful in this endeavour. Despite the gloom in the critiques of the biodiversity convention outlined above, there is never a questioning of the formulation of the problem of biodiversity loss itself. The implication is that this this is someone else's task – or rather some other discipline from the natural sciences.

A genealogy of the biodiversity convention: description of method

What if, instead, the legal scholar is not satisfied with the *a priori* of environmental problems handed to them by the sciences? What if the problem(s) is never closed? What if they take into account the notion that biodiversity as an idea has its own history and is distinct from, but also irrevocably bound with, the legal history of the biodiversity convention? For that matter, what if there are different ways to write the history of that idea and convention? What if they dig deeper into all of this, using a particular tool, that of genealogy, adapted to the task of explaining the paradox of the undead convention? First, this would present a challenge to the very conception of how a problem is constituted and rendered intelligible for international environmental law. Second, this move would add to our understanding of the operation of the biodiversity convention.

Legal genealogy[72] is a form of inquiry that proceeds by historicizing and destabilizing certain categories of legal thought and objects of legal analysis. The method is largely adapted from the original work of Michel Foucault[73] and subsequent interpretations and applications.[74] Genealogy is a critical form of inquiry, in that it aims to denaturalize, destabilize, and render contingent these legal categories and objects, by excavating their past and historicizing them. Genealogical historicization thus sets the basis for genealogical contestation, that is, for a genealogical critique of law. According to Ben Golder:

> A legal genealogy is a form of historical inquiry that, written from the vantage of the present and emphasizing the contingency and non-necessary status of that present, seeks to demonstrate how a legal object or practice emerged and came to be. In emphasizing contingency, such a historical method problematizes the notion of a singular, determinate origin and challenges totalizing forms of historical narration.[75]

This historicization of the present proceeds through the use of multiple processes of problematization, a methodological tool developed in Foucault's later work.[76] The approach identifies a category of legal thought or a legal object that constitutes a problem in the present, and seeks to trace its genealogy, i.e., trace how it came to be understood in the way it is presently understood.[77] In the case at hand, this problem is the biodiversity convention. An explanation for its paradoxical persistence is being sought, through this genealogical approach. As the quote from Golder above suggests, this first problematization brings about a second problematization, where the stable, universal understanding of this legal object – i.e., the biodiversity convention – within the field is challenged, precisely by revealing the process of its formulation as such a legal object.

Problematization thus entails a key reversal of historical focus; one is not examining solutions or past alternatives to draw lessons from, but the problems themselves that gave rise to these solutions. It entails a focus on the ways phenomena, behaviours, actions, processes, discourses, and the like are rendered problematic; how they become conceived as a problem requiring a solution;[78] the solution in question being the signing of an international agreement, the creation of a treaty regime, and its continued operation over a number of decades.

In short, then, 'genealogies articulate problems'.[79] A problem, for the purposes of this genealogical schema, has the specific meaning of a problem of government, meaning a problem that represents a target for governmental intervention by some combination of policy, law, regulation, and governance. In the context of a legal enquiry, the use of problematization collapses the law and politics distinction. Problematization can then be defined in the broadest of terms as the conceptualization of reality into an object of governmental thought. It provides the 'terms of reference within which an issue is cast'.[80] A proposal of such solutions to a problem, such as the creation of new international institutions, regimes, and strategic plans is made possible by problematizations that link the real-world problems with the solutions.

This is not simply a matter of the expression, representation, or manifestation of reality into abstract, legal, or political discourse; 'in connection with them, [problematization] develops the conditions in which possible responses can be given; it defines the elements that will constitute what the different solutions attempt to respond to'.[81] Problematization is not simply representation, but creates a grid of legible responses that are considered rational. It is a form of governmental thought that structures the possibility of a range of valid and legitimate solutions – new, different, or reformed behaviours, actions, processes, institutions, discourses – that can be derived from a particular framing of a problem of government.

By setting out these problematizations, genealogy can then proceed to the solutions that emerge in response to or provoked by these problematizations. Foucault identifies this second, corresponding unit of the genealogical methodological schema with the term of *practices*. This term serves to emphasize the methodological point that problematizations are not representations of reality

The 'undead' convention 13

based on ideas or a particular ideology, but emerge from these practices.[82] Practices are understood by Foucault 'as places where what is said and what is done, rules imposed and reasons given, the planned and the taken for granted meet and interconnect'.[83] Koopman defines Foucault's practices as 'complex compositions of techniques, beliefs, styles, powers, knowledges, and ethics... emerging in and through problematizations and the reconstructive responses provoked by these problematizations'.[84] For example, the advent of goal and target setting in international law, which has reached the biodiversity convention, can be considered as one such practice, in response to concerns over accountable governance.[85]

Assembled together, these practices form 'regimes of practices', that is, 'programmes of conduct which have both prescriptive effects regarding what is to be done (effects of "jurisdiction"), and codifying effects regarding what is to be known (effects of "veridiction")'.[86] A *programme* is 'a set of calculated, reasoned prescriptions in terms of which institutions are meant to be recognized, spaces arranged, and behaviours regulated'.[87] It is thus, in the terminology of this book, a governmental programme. Genetic gold is considered in the analysis presented in subsequent chapters as one such programme.

A programme thus can pre-exist a given problematization (that precisely seeks to problematize such a programme) and/or emerge or be shaped by it (as a solution). Genealogy's excavation of the past becomes a multi-layered investigation into the conditions that enabled the emergence of certain practices and programmes as solutions to certain problems, into how these proposed solutions problematize their targets in the first place, and, thirdly, into the assumptions derived from this problematization to which these solutions are designed to respond.

Practices and problematizations, intricately linked, imbricated in forming the conditions of their mutual and contingent emergence and co-existence. As compositions of diverse elements, mutually reinforcing as they intersect and coalesce into assembled programmes, they formulate and disperse based on reformulations of the problematizations that modify the conditions of possibility for their emergence. What constitutes a valid or legitimate proposal (of practices, norms, principles, institutions, rules, actions, behaviours, etc.) to address a problem is already framed by the understanding of what constitutes a problem in the first place. Traditional categories and objects of legal analysis are thus subsumed within this complex schema. In effect, the stable, fixed objects of legal inquiry (jurisdiction, treaty, institution, etc.) are replaced by *relations*.[88] There is no rationality external to a particular problematization of some aspect of the real world.

Problems and solutions, ideas, theories, institutions – traditional categories and objects of analysis – thus become recast within a genealogical schema of problematizations, practices, and programmes. From a practical methodological perspective, accessing these problematizations, practices, and programmes is undertaken through the study of regulations, policy guides, popularizations

14 The 'undead' convention

into applied science (books written for a popular audience), what Foucault called 'practical' or 'prescriptive texts', 'whose main object is to suggest rules of conduct'.[89] This approach facilitates the reading of legal texts (academic commentary, treaties, decisions, resolutions, and the like) within an interdisciplinary context. In the chapters that follow, these texts are placed side by side with texts from a host of other disciplines, read and interpreted in the same exact manner, from the perspective of the problematization they frame. In this way, this genealogy examines how past conservation practices and environmental problematizations in relation to nature and life were 'governmentalized', that is, problematized as the bases for the emergence of a solution from the field of international law in the shape of a multilateral biodiversity convention. These accounts constitute a core element of this book.

A genealogy of problematizations, therefore, is a history of a particular form of thought. The term 'thought' is used here in this governmental sense, following Foucault, to distinguish genealogy from the history of ideas;[90] 'this was the proper task of a history of thought, as against the history of behaviours or representations: to define the conditions in which human beings "problematize" what they are, what they do, and the world in which they live'.[91] The creation of the whole field of international environmental law, and its individual conventions and regimes, can thus be conceptualized as practices and programmes intrinsically linked to problematizations.

Methodological concerns

Employing a Foucaultian genealogical approach must come with a series of caveats. It is, by now, heavily burdened with the weight of decades of widespread and loosely defined application across the humanities and social sciences. It has become a 'somewhat trendy label in academia… as if anyone who does history is not themselves a historian is eager to describe their work as a "genealogy"'.[92] In legal studies, in particular, some form of historicization and a broad genealogical 'orientation' have 'become almost axiomatic within vast swathes of contemporary critical legal thought'.[93] Genealogy's excavation of the past thus has to proceed with care, clarity, and precision, lest one assumes the role of the proverbial Professor Challenger and digs too wantonly.

I address four major concerns regarding the genealogical approach, as it applies to law. The first concern is the contentious relationship between genealogy and history, and the transposition of this relation into the legal field. The second relates to the decreasing critical potency of the finding of contingency, often promoted by genealogy. The third concern relates to a similar decrease in the critical force of the finding of a 'masked power', i.e., of the political hiding behind formal law, also brought on by the widespread use of the genealogical approach. Finally, I argue that a focus on genealogy as a methodological approach protects the work from a fetishization of Foucault himself as the political philosopher *par excellence*.

The first concern relates to the relation between genealogy and history.[94] Legal genealogy is generally critical of mainstream approaches to the history of international law, underpinned by a teleological historical understanding. Legal genealogy is not another form of legal history, and genealogical historicization is distinct from other forms of historical enquiries into law. This is because it does not subscribe to the historiographical idea of the historical evolution of ideas, values, institutions, or practices, characterized by some form of immanent progressive reason and developing teleologically towards the present. Its units of analysis are problems, practices, and programmes, and their interplay. Genealogy is thus directly opposed to the inherent teleology that international environmental law has adopted for itself.[95]

The connection between legal history and the idea of precedent or the viewing of history through the lens of establishing legal precedent is also opposed by genealogy. Precedent establishes stability and legitimacy, both of the legal object and category in question, as well as law as a field and method. Genealogy has no interest, acknowledged or unacknowledged, in establishing such credentials through the accumulation of historical evidence. Instead, genealogy focuses on contingent emergence[96] – local, provisional, contested, and unstable – and the various breaks that precipitate such forms of emergence.

The second concern relates to the fetishization of contingency in scholarship. Showing that our present is 'contingent' and has a history, or that structures, institutions, and values previously thought of as stable and universal are nothing of the sort no longer appears as a particularly critical or radical move. The trope and manoeuvre of 'destabilizing' the present, prevalent in genealogy-flavoured critical scholarship, emerges as a lazy, pernicious, destructive, political dead-end in our contemporary world, where there are plenty of voices, in media and politics, let alone academia, willing to wallow or bask in the darkness of a chaotic, disintegrating late modernity and world order. We do not live in what seems like a particularly or excessively stable world. The most prescient of scholars had realized this blind spot long before our current age of pandemics, post-truth, and generalized anger.[97]

Exposing contingency, therefore, is not what it used to be. Yet genealogy can still have a critical effect if care is taken with the choice of objects towards which it is directed. Not all legal objects of critique are created equal, Golder reminds us; some 'are rather more invested in...their sense of timeless self-evidence and necessity than others'.[98] The sense of universalism and urgency that characterizes the field of international environmental law, and its objects, such as biodiversity, makes them particularly suited to a genealogical critique that would expose the contingent construction of such understandings. Genealogy stands as an obstacle to their continuous and manic hurtling towards a future, fuelled by historical assumptions about their self-constitution as necessary and self-evident responses to global problems.[99] It is the force of such conceptions that produces paradoxes, such as that of the undead convention that animates this book.

16 The 'undead' convention

The crucial element of a properly structured genealogy is not to simply show that the present has a history, is contingent, and could be otherwise; but to show *how* this contingent present has emerged and *how* it could be otherwise.[100] The latter, however, does not mean that a fully formed 'alternative' to the present can be found in the past, only that the past provides sources for rethinking the present. Bewitched by the false emancipatory potential of contingency, genealogies are often understood to be looking in the past for 'alternatives' to our contemporary categories, institutions, and values, committing the fallacy of presentism. This goes against Foucault's own conception of his genealogical project: 'you can't find the solution of a problem in the solution of another problem raised at another moment by other people.'[101]

The third concern relates to the 'masking' of power. The genealogical contestation adopted in this book is distinguished from most of the genealogical work within the field of critical legal theory. The latter belongs to what Colin Koopman calls 'biopower-hunting' scholarship, whose methodological procedure 'seems to be that of fettering out the nefarious hidden workings of biopower (or disciplinary power, or slavish morality) in some context where its appearance was perhaps unexpected'.[102] But to claim, for example, that power and knowledge underpin international environmental law and global environmental governance is not particularly critical. It is rather trite by this point. In addition to contingency, we are also past the trashing stage and the 'hermeneutics of suspicion'[103] critique. There is no need for elaborate theoretical apparatus to articulate and support such a claim. Demonstrating the detail of how this has occurred (and, indeed, how power and knowledge came together), however, is still useful, in order to imagine how it could be otherwise. Genealogy unpacks and presents all the 'parts' that make up the 'engine' that drives the self-constitution and self-belief of/in a field such as international environmental law. This is implemented with the proviso that this is not another version of tearing down, trashing, or power-hunting. Given contemporary conditions, genealogy should not lightly and unreflexively join in what has perniciously been called in some quarters the 'postmodernist dance of death on the grave of universal values'.[104] It would be easy to use critique to trash the biodiversity convention and support its dissolution. That would solve the paradox of the undead convention by aligning the reality of failure with a discourse of failure, closing the book on the convention. The genealogical approach adopted here will instead enable us to understand and explain this paradox.

The fourth concern relates to the reception and influence of Michel Foucault in academic circles. It is important to underline that legal genealogy is precisely a methodology; a diagnostic and analytical toolkit.[105] Foucault himself, of course, did use genealogy to great effect, deriving influential new concepts from his inquiries, such as biopolitics, discipline, and governmentality. These concepts are the product of the application of a particular methodology to address his particular enquiries. Yet they often appear to uncritically travel with genealogy as unacknowledged intellectual baggage. Such a methodological move transforms the work from Foucaultian to *Foucaultianist*. It consists of a Foucaultian terminological onslaught approximating, through its sheer linguistic mass, some form of orthodox philosophical doctrine and political theory all rolled into one. But the transfer of genealogy over to the legal field should not equate automatically with the additional transfer of Foucault's elaborate conceptual apparatus that was developed from his inquiries and methodologies.[106] The following should then be underlined: genealogical historicization, and by extension, contestation and critique is transferred into the legal field because it is argued to be an effective methodological schema for legal enquiry, rather than a parroting of a certain *Foucaultianism*. This clarification serves to distinguish the theoretical framework of this particular approach from its trendy applications within the broader theoretical field, under which it invariably will be housed.

The analytics of environmental reason

The biodiversity convention is an apt target for a genealogical approach because it is a legal object heavily invested in its own sense of ahistorical necessity and urgency, as well as universality. The treaty regime is irrevocably bound to the crisis of global biodiversity in decline; requiring urgent global action in the present, to safeguard the future. It appears invested in producing even more universally accepted 'global deals on nature'.[107] The continued operation of the biodiversity convention and its burgeoning treaty regime appears incongruous to its ultimate lack of effect in terms of arresting global biodiversity decline, a gap between rhetoric and reality that increases after each successive strategic plan.

The historicization of biodiversity and the related international agreement is not an end in itself; nor is the aim to critique the biodiversity convention from a historical perspective, or to locate something pure and forgotten in the origins of the idea of biodiversity that will somehow save this undead convention and make it relevant and effective again. The biodiversity convention does possess a history as a revolving assemblage of problematizations, practices, and programmes, an account that is different from the mainstream legal history of the evolution of an international environmental treaty.

The past holds no fully fledged alternatives; just the elements of what become a composite environmental reason within the structure of international environmental law. Heterogeneous ideas of biodiversity, at various junctures attempting to co-opt, alter, and manipulate biodiversity towards different strategic goals and regulatory interventions, can be located through their use in projects of government, by using the genealogical framework outlined in this chapter. By gathering and organising problematizations, practices, and programmes together, a genealogy is, however, able to define and present a system of thought, a form of rationality or reason[108] that underpins the deployment of international law to address biodiversity decline.

18 The 'undead' convention

Like problems, programmes are understood as programmes of government. They constitute the practices that they problematize so that they become amenable to governing.[109] They provide the grid of intelligibility and permissibility, a basis upon which a particular governmental thought can flourish; a basis for judging, evaluating, regulating;[110] ultimately, governing. Programmes are directly opposed to the notion of scientific *a priori* that environmental law espouses; they are not objective solutions to a pre-formed problem that is external to this thought. They instead bind together the two parts of the normative proposition 'this, then needs to be done', casting the frame, range, and scale for what can be considered a workable solution; what Foucault called effects of 'veridiction'. Following this schema, we can observe how an object of legal thought is a much more constrained entity compared to an object of governmental thought, produced by a specific programme. The goal of a genealogy is to cast the former into the broader terms of the latter; to contextualize international law within a broader logic or *reason* of government.

Genealogy thus gives access to this governmental thought. It is this biodiversity reason that explains the paradox of the undead convention because it charts the emergence of the multiple relations that give rise to and support its continuing operation. In particular, the programme of genetic gold will be examined as a key element of the genealogy of the biodiversity convention.

Since the convention is broadly considered the response to an environmental problem of biodiversity loss, the analysis will begin with the problem of biodiversity loss itself. But this time, there will be no neat closure of the problem supporting a clear, and mutually reinforcing, division between ecology and law. There will be no problem of biodiversity loss to briefly describe and move on, but a problematization of biodiversity loss; in fact, a whole series of these problematizations will be presented in the next chapters; problematizations that languish, contradict, and reverberate with each other over decades.

Notes

1 Title of a press release by the CBD secretariat https://www.cbd.int/doc/press/2010/pr-2010-10-06-ci-en.pdf.
2 Don De Lillo, *Underworld* (1997).
3 UNEP/CBD/EXCOP 1/Decision EM-I.3 (2000), Annex.
4 UNEP/CBD/COP/10/Decision X.1 (2010), Annex.
5 UNEP/CBD/COP/10/Decision BS-V/11 (2010), Annex.
6 Philippe G. Le Prestre (ed), *Governing Global Biodiversity: The Evolution and Implementation of the Convention on Biological Diversity* (Routledge 2002), 5.
7 CBD, Art. 2.
8 CBD, Art. 3 and 4.
9 CBD, Art. 1.
10 Except indirectly in certain provisions of the Preamble.
11 Patricia Birnie and others, *International Law and the Environment* (3rd edn, Oxford University Press 2009), 616.

12 CBD, Art. 8.

13 CBD, Preamble.

14 Eric Dinerstein and others, 'An Ecoregion-Based Approach to Protecting Half the Terrestrial Realm' (2017) 67 *BioScience* 534, 534; Bernard Coetzee and others, 'Local Scale Comparisons of Biodiversity as a Test for Global Protected Area Ecological Performance: A Meta-Analysis' (2014) 9 *PloS one* e105824, 1.

15 Further discussed later in this chapter.

16 Strategic Goal C, Target 11.

17 CBD, Art. 9.

18 CBD, Art. 2.

19 David M. Ong, 'International Environmental Law Governing Threats to Biodiversity' in Malgosia Fitzmaurice and others (eds), *Research Handbook on International Environmental Law* (Edward Elgar 2010), 534.

20 Edith Brown Weiss, 'In Fairness to Future Generations and Sustainable Development' (1992) *American University Journal of International Law and Policy* 19.

21 Nagoya Protocol, Art. 2.

22 CBD, Art. 2.

23 CBD, Art. 2.

24 '"Derivative" means a naturally occurring biochemical compound resulting from the genetic expression or metabolism of biological or genetic resources, even if it does not contain functional units of heredity'. See Nagoya Protocol, Art. 2.

25 CBD, Art. 19.

26 CBD, Art. 8(j), 15, 16, and 19.

27 CBD, Art. 8(j).

28 Ong, 534.

29 Alan E. Boyle, 'The Rio Convention on Biological Diversity' in Catherine Redgwell and Michael Bowman (eds), *International Law and the Conservation of Biological Diversity* (Kluwer Law International 1995), 37.

30 Birnie and others, 617.

31 CBD, Art. 6.

32 CBD, Art. 26.

33 Simon Lyster, *International Wildlife Law: An Analysis of International Treaties Concerned with the Conservation of Wildlife* (Grotius 1985).

34 Convention on Nature Protection and Wildlife Preservation in the Western Hemisphere (1940), 161 UNTS 103.

35 Lyster (n.2), 111. This characterization has been maintained in the newer edition. See Michael Bowman and others, *Lyster's International Wildlife Law* (2nd edn, Cambridge University Press 2010), 242.

36 CBD, Art. 23.

37 CBD, Art. 24. This function is performed by UNEP.

38 UNEP/CBD/COP/12/Decision XII.26 (2012).

39 CBD, Art. 25.

40 On agricultural, dry, and sub-humid lands, forest, inland waters, island, marine and coastal, and mountain biodiversity.

41 Such as impact assessment, invasive alien species, and many others. More information available at: https://www.cbd.int/programmes/.

42 UNEP/CBD/COP/12/Decision XII.27 (2012).

43 For a list of UN agencies, intergovernmental and nongovernmental organizations, industry, and universities, observers, and participants at the most recent COP, see *Report of the Conference of the Parties to the Convention on Biological Diversity on its Fourteenth Meeting.* UNEP/CBD/COP/14/14, Annex I.

20 The 'undead' convention

44 A provision used by the US to maintain observer status, despite its rejection of the treaty.

45 'Any other body or agency, whether governmental or non-governmental, qualified in fields relating to conservation and sustainable use of biological diversity, which has informed the Secretariat of its wish to be represented as an observer at a meeting of the Conference of the Parties, may be admitted unless at least one third of the Parties present object.' See CBD, Art. 23(5).

46 Edith Brown Weiss, 'International Environmental Law: Contemporary Issues and the Emergence of a New World Order' (1993) 81 *Geo LJ* 675, 684.

47 Geoffrey Palmer, 'New ways to make international environmental law' (1992) 86 *American Journal of International Law* 259

48 Don Anton, 'Treaty Congestion in International Environmental Law' in Erika J. Techera (ed), *Routledge Handbook of International Environmental Law* (Routledge 2012).

49 Joanna Depledge, 'The Opposite of Learning: Ossification in the Climate Change Regime' (2006) 6 *Global Environmental Politics* 1.

50 Lavanya Rajamani, 'From Stockholm to Johannesburg: The Anatomy of Dissonance in the International Environmental Dialogue' (2003) 12 *Review of European Community and International Environmental Law* 23.

51 David M. Driesen, 'Thirty Years of International Environmental Law: A Retrospective and Plea for Reinvigoration' (2003) 30 *Syracuse J Int'l L & Com* 353.

52 Daniel Bodansky, *The Art and Craft of International Environmental Law* (Harvard University Press 2010), 35.

53 UNGA Res 61/203 (2006).

54 The Strategic Plan for Biodiversity 2011–2020 and the Aichi Biodiversity Targets '*Living in Harmony with* Nature', see UNEP/CBD/COP/10/Decision X.2 (2010), Annex.

55 UNGA Res 65/161 (2010).

56 Title of a 2010 press release by the Secretariat of the Biodiversity Convention, referring to the CBD's second strategic plan. Available at: https://www.cbd.int/doc/press/2010/pr-2010-10-29-cop-10-en.pdf.

57 'If Kyoto entered history as the city where the climate accord was born, Nagoya will be remembered as the city where the biodiversity accord was born.' Ibid.

58 The title is directly borrowed from George Monbiot, 'A Ghost Agreement' (The Guardian 2 November 2010).

59 'Strategic Plan for The Convention on Biological Diversity', see UNEP/CBD/COP 6/Decision VI.26 (2002), Annex.

60 As Target 7.B.

61 'Living in Harmony with Nature' (n.54), par. 7.

62 CBD, *Global Biodiversity Outlook 3* (2010), 9.

63 Nor will other environmental goals of a similar nature be met 'under current trajectories'. See IPBES, 'Summary for policymakers of the global assessment report on biodiversity and ecosystem services of the Intergovernmental Science-Policy Platform on Biodiversity and Ecosystem Services' (2019), 6–7.

64 The issues surrounding this protocol are analyzed in Chapter 5.

65 'Living in Harmony with Nature' (n.54), par. 11.

66 E.g., UNEP/CBD/COP/14/Decision 14/34 (2018).

67 Ibid.

68 A. Dan Tarlock, 'Who Owns Science?' (2002) 10 *Penn State Environmental Law Review* 135; John McEldowney and Sharron McEldowney, 'Science and Environmental Law: Collaboration across the Double Helix' (2011) 13 *Environmental Law Review* 169.

The 'undead' convention   21

69 David B. Schorr, 'Historical Analysis in Environmental Law' in Markus B. Dubber and Cristopher Tomlins (eds), *The Oxford Handbook of Legal History* (Oxford University Press 2018).

70 Philippe G. Le Prestre, 'Introduction: The Emergence of Global Biodiversity Governance' in Philippe G. Le Prestre (ed), *Governing Global Biodiversity: The Evolution and Implementation of the Convention on Biological Diversity* (Routledge 2002), 3.

71 Andreas Philippopoulos-Mihalopoulos, 'Looking for the Space between Law and Ecology' in Andreas Philippopoulos-Mihalopoulos (ed), *Law and Ecology: New Environmental Legal Foundations* (Routledge 2011); Andreas Philippopoulos-Mihalopoulos, '"...The Sound of Breaking String": Critical Environmental Law and Ontological Vulnerability' (2011) 2 *Journal of Human Rights and the Environment* 5.

72 The method is partly based in the interpretation found in Ben Golder, 'Contemporary Legal Genealogies' in Justin Desautels-Stein and Cristopher Tomlins (eds), *Searching for Contemporary Legal Thought* (Cambridge University Press 2017).

73 A clear and effective example of the genealogical approach in action can be found in Michel Foucault, *The Will to Knowledge: The History of Sexuality Volume 1* (Penguin 1998 [1976]).

74 See generally Colin Koopman, *Genealogy as Critique: Foucault and the Problems of Modernity* (Indiana University Press 2013).

75 Golder (n.72), 83.

76 Problematization features in a reorientation of genealogy after the publication of the first volume of *The History of Sexuality* in 1976. This reorientation, in line with previous changes in direction by Foucault, is malleable and takes many forms, as recounted in Michel Foucault, 'Polemics, Politics and Problematizations' in Paul Rabinow (ed), *Ethics: Subjectivity and Truth* (Penguin 2000); Michel Foucault, 'On the Genealogy of Ethics: An Overview of a Work in Progress' in Paul Rabinow (ed), *The Foucault Reader: An Introduction to Foucault's Thought* (Penguin 1991). For a reworked presentation of problematization as a method see Michel Foucault, *The Use of Pleasure: The History of Sexuality Volume 2* (Penguin 1992 [1984]). Towards the end of his life, Foucault ultimately claimed that 'what serves as a form of work common to the work I've done since *Madness and Civilization* is the notion of problematization'. Michel Foucault, 'The Concern for Truth' in Lawrence D. Kritzman (ed), *Michel Foucault Politics, Philosophy, Culture: Interviews and Other Writings 1977–1984* (Routledge 1988), 257.

77 'I set out from a problem expressed in the terms current today and try to work out its genealogy. Genealogy means that I begin my analysis from a question posed in the present'. Foucault, 'The Concern for Truth' (n.76), 262.

78 Michel Foucault, *Fearless Speech* (Semiotext(e) 2001), 171; Foucault, *The Use of Pleasure: The History of Sexuality Volume 2* (n.76), 10–11.

79 Koopman (n.74), 1.

80 Carol Bacchi, 'Why Study Problematizations? Making Politics Visible' (2012) 2 *Open Journal of Political Science* 1, 1.

81 Foucault, 'Polemics, Politics and Problematizations' (n.76), 389.

82 Foucault, *The Use of Pleasure: The History of Sexuality Volume 2* (n.76), 11–12.

83 Michel Foucault, 'Questions of Method' in Graham Burchell and others (eds), *The Foucault Effect: Studies in Governmentality* (The University of Chicago Press 1991), 75.

84 Koopman (n.74), 101.

85 Frank Biermann and others, 'Global Governance by Goal-Setting: The Novel Approach of the UN Sustainable Development Goals' (2017) 26–27 *Current Opinion in Environmental Sustainability* 26.

86 Foucault, 'Questions of Method' (n.83), 75.

87 See ibid 80.

88 Paul Veyne, 'Foucault Revolutionizes History' in Arnold I. Davidson (ed), *Foucault and His Interlocutors* (University of Chicago Press 1997), 181.

89 Foucault, *The Use of Pleasure: The History of Sexuality Volume 2* (n.76), 12–13.

90 Foucault defines the former as the 'analysis of systems of representation' and the latter as the 'analysis of attitudes and types of action' in Foucault, 'Polemics, Politics and Problematizations' (n.76), 388.

91 Foucault, *The Use of Pleasure: The History of Sexuality Volume 2* (n.76), 10.

92 Koopman (n.74), 5.

93 Golder (n.72), 80.

94 Jan Goldstein (ed), *Foucault and the Writing of History* (Blackwell 1994).

95 E.g., Peter H. Sand, 'The Evolution of International Environmental Law' in Daniel Bodansky and others (eds), *The Oxford Handbook of International Environmental Law* (OUP 2007).

96 Michel Foucault, 'Nietzsche, Genealogy, History' in James D. Faubion (ed), *Aesthetics, Method and Espistemology: Essential Works of Foucault 1954–1984 Volume 2* (Penguin 2000), 83.

97 Golder (n.72), 88–94 discusses the work of Nikolas Rose, Christopher Tomlins, and Susan Marks highlighting the dangers of such critical scholarship.

98 Ibid 80.

99 As elaborated *supra*.

100 Koopman (n.74), 130.

101 Foucault, 'On the Genealogy of Ethics: An Overview of a Work in Progress', 343.

102 Koopman (n.74), 6.

103 Brian Leiter, 'The Hermeneutics of Suspicion: Recovering Marx, Nietzsche and Freud' in Brian Leiter (ed), *The Future of Philosophy* (Oxford University Press 2004).

104 Mitchell Dean, *Governmentality: Power and Rule in Modern Society* (2nd edn, Sage 2010), 57.

105 Koopman (n.74), 6–7.

106 On this distinction see Colin Koopman and Tomas Matza, 'Putting Foucault to Work: Analytic and Concept in Foucaultian Inquiry' (2013) 39 *Critical Inquiry* 817.

107 More recently, the 2020 strategic plan has adopted this mantle, although the Nagoya conference outcomes of 2010 was also described as such, as discussed *supra*.

108 Foucault describes his work along these lines in Michel Foucault, 'What is Called "Punishing"?' in James D. Faubion (ed), *Power: Essential Works of Focault 1954–1984 Volume Three* (Penguin 2002), 383.

109 Roger Deacon, 'Theory as Practice: Foucault's Concept of Problematization' (2000) 118 *Telos* 127, 132.

110 Thomas Flynn, 'Foucault's Mapping of History' in Gary Gutting (ed), *The Cambridge Companion to Foucault* (2nd edn, Cambridge University Press 2003), 31.

Chapter 2

Lambswool into synthetic
Early programmes

The toxic event had released a spirit of imagination. People spun tales, others listened spellbound.

There was a growing respect for the vivid rumour, the most chilling tale. We were no closer to believing or disbelieving a given story than we had been earlier.

But there was a greater appreciation.

We began to marvel at our own ability to manufacture awe.[1]

The term 'biological diversity' and its widely established contraction into 'biodiversity' experienced a meteoric rise onto the forefront of environmental discourse in the short span of ten years, between the mid-1980s and the mid-1990s. It was 'transformed from a bit of scientific esoterica into a buzzword of popular culture'.[2] The rise, at least in terms of academic interest, continued into the early to mid-2000s.[3] The buzz is now gone; academic interest and popular consciousness have moved on. This is now the backwater of academic research and environmental politics, a submerged milieu that this genealogy begins to explore, starting with invention of term in a series of prescriptive texts in the fields of ecology and conservation.

Before its current diffusion across the environmental domain, the concept of an inherent natural or biological diversity in need of protection was first proposed within work striving for some balance between the theories of ecology and biology and the practices of nature conservation. At a superficial level, one can talk of a shift in terminology, from nature conservation to biodiversity conservation. In addition to this obvious terminological shift established in the late 1980s, there is also the shift from the full biological diversity to the contracted biodiversity to be examined. The 'scientific esoterica' of biological diversity and the buzzword of biodiversity are different sides of an effort to frame nature conservation as a problem of government requiring significant changes, first in the regime of conservation practices and then more broadly within society. These shifts were just indications of a broader transformation, eventually leading to the articulation of new, integrative, but multi-threaded

24 Lambswool into synthetic

environmental discourses that connected previously separate ecological and conservation problematizations.

Biological diversity before biodiversity

Core elements of what would eventually become biodiversity can be found in the work of Norman Moore, the British conservationist well-known for his work at the Nature Conservancy's Monks Wood experimentation station exposing the harmful effects of organochlorine pesticides such as DDT on birds.[4] In a 1969 article, he argues for a programme where 'conservation of diversity should be the primary aim of conservation'.[5] Moore was concerned with the lack of overarching aim and rationality for conservation practice and outlined how the idea of biological diversity could assist in rectifying this crucial gap. In this work, biological diversity emerges as a programme for change in response to a problematization of conservation practices.

Moore's research is focused on the hazardous effects of certain pesticides, but he acknowledges that it forms part of a 'general complex of interacting problems, which includes the human population explosion, increased exploitation of land, rapid technological advance, and environmental pollution'.[6] Arguments in favour of conservation would have to be formulated with this complex in mind, and, in particular, the attitudes towards nature of the people that form this complex. He generally found such attitudes wanting, whether it is the notion of nature as landscape – background to human activity, the notion of a natural balance, the lack of understanding of persistent versus catastrophic pollution, and, most pointedly, 'the fragmented view of Man and Nature', reflected in the 'multiplicity of organizations of which each tends to take a narrow sectoral interest in whole problems'.[7]

Moore's problematization of such attitudes towards nature serve to underlie the further problematization of attitudes towards, as well as the regime of, conservation practice in itself; both of which he finds equally wanting. The list of faulty attitudes and practices is equally long, including the understanding of conservation as an activity focused on preserving rare plants and animals, and which has spiritual, aesthetic, and intellectual roots, as opposed to an instrumental aim. Conservation is also understood as 'a negative activity concerned with protecting the past, rather than a positive one concerned with providing for the future'.[8] Moore's problematizations are damning for both 'ecologically trained' conservationists and other people. The latter are 'ecologically illiterate' and their mentality is deficient due to lack of knowledge, while the former have failed to propose 'an acceptable philosophy and rationale for conservation'.[9]

Moore's proposal involves moving from rarity (of 'special' species) to diversity (of the whole): '[conservationists] should be explicit that their fundamental aim is to conserve biological diversity either for its own sake or for the future good of mankind.'[10] Although biological diversity is not defined explicitly, it is thought to provide 'an understandable and coordinating purpose underlying all conservation activities', but pointedly not 'a blueprint for detailed action'.[11] Biological diversity thus establishes an overarching aim and rationale of protecting the 'whole', to which specific priorities and activities are to relate. Moore believes that 'if we can give a rational basis for the choice of our priorities, we can hope to enlist much greater support for conservation activities'.[12] Biological diversity thus is to provide guidance for organising and administering conservation practices towards more holistic and instrumental aims, so as to increase support for them within society.

This overarching aim, based on the idea of the 'Earth as an integrated whole',[13] is the prioritization of conserving whole ecosystems, instead of separate, individual species and organisms. According to Moore, given that there are millions of the latter, the most effective way to protect them is to conserve a sufficient diversity of different habitats housing a sufficient diversity of species. In this argument, different aspects of diversity, i.e., species and habitat or ecosystem diversity, emerge both as concepts, as well as targets for conservation practices. The rationality also accepts the spatial limitations of the practice of conservation of habitats through natural reserves. Therefore, the general logic is complemented by a focus on specific species of special economic, scientific, or aesthetic value.[14] These would be subject to special conservation measures.

The programme that Moore proposes, through the vehicle of biological diversity, has direct implications for the relation between conservation and society. Biological diversity was 'an unplanned by-product of the world in which we lived'[15] – that is, unplanned by humanity. This is no longer the case in the mid-20th century. Given the pressures from the human population, effective conservation can only be *active* conservation, and benign neglect of reserves will not work: 'we shall only conserve what we plan to keep and what we pay in both effort and money.'[16] Biological diversity is – or rather will have to be – a *planned* product of applied human knowledge of the environment and conservation practices.

In addition, conservation will have to compete economically with other activities, yet Moore does not believe that a comprehensive economic assessment of nature is possible; substitute indicators, such as land value, need to be used.[17] Even more challenging will be the conservation of biological diversity outside nature reserves, where it will have to compete directly with other land uses, such as agriculture. Moore here uses his own experience in efforts to control the use of certain pesticides to demonstrate 'how vulnerable the conservation interest [is] unless it coincides with a more generally accepted interest'.[18]

The aim of the conservation of biological diversity is, in the end, translated into a programme that consists of three main strategic objectives: (i) the acquisition of nature reserves; (ii) a targeted, tactical approach whereby conservation measures are supported only in conjunction with other human interests; and (iii) some commonly accepted valuable species receiving special treatment. An acknowledged corollary of such a programme is that certain species and habitats are to be abandoned due to the interests and needs of human society.

26 Lambswool into synthetic

Moore's biological diversity is presented as a pragmatic guide to rear-guard political action to be taken by 'conservationists' depicted as an enlightened social group that ultimately represents a minority view.[19] Conservation exists and is problematized within the complex of problems of human society he outlines in the beginning of this article, and cannot be considered in isolation from these problems and activities. Although certain attitudes and aspects of society are found to be problematic, there is no consideration or intimation of a programme of change related to them. Society is fixed; it is conservation that needs to adapt to its realities. Biological diversity as an overarching aim appears to be focused on addressing problems within conservation practice, with a view to convincing human society of its merits as a worthwhile activity and investment. Moore's pragmatic environmental reason has to adjust to a pre-existing and fixed political reason. It is about getting one's house in order in anticipation of guests arriving.

Considered a 'seminal'[20] work in the invention of contemporary biodiversity, the second chapter in the Council on Environmental Quality (CEQ)'s *Eleventh Annual Report*, compiled by Elliot Norse and Roger McManus in 1980,[21] is notable for presenting the first conception of biological diversity as consisting of a hierarchy of distinct components requiring combined protection under a single conservation objective. In line with CEQ's role within the implementation of US environmental law and policy,[22] the report was a policy document that attempted a mapping of major environmental problems and provided a comprehensive assessment of the US administrations' efforts to address those, as well as recommendations and guidance for future environmental law and policy initiatives. The chapter in question consistently seeks to outline problematic regimes of practices in response to its newly invented problematization of biological diversity.

Norse later recounted that they were tasked with the 'unprecedented subject of the status of life on Earth'.[23] Although there was growing concern with accelerating species extinction, similar concerns were being expressed about the degradation of whole ecosystems, as well as the availability of germplasm resources for maintaining the health of agricultural crops and the world's food supply. A synthesis of such conservation concerns was required and was ultimately expressed in this chapter through the medium of biological diversity, a 'term that encompassed all that was being lost'.[24] Here, biological diversity did not represent a problematization of aimless, unscientific, and un-strategic conservation, as was the case in Moore, but a problematization of humanity's adverse impact on nature, and by extension, the ensuing impact of this generalized loss on society.

In the chapter, biological diversity is defined as including:

> two related concepts, genetic diversity and ecological diversity. Genetic diversity is the amount of genetic variability among individuals in a single species...Ecological diversity (species richness) is the number of species in a community of organisms.[25]

Both are described as 'fundamental in the functioning of ecological systems'.[26] The chapter stops short of identifying a third level of ecosystem diversity, which would subsequently be added. This latter addition is reflected in the legal definition of biodiversity enshrined in the CBD text.

The CEQ chapter sets out the value of this biological diversity, which is based on the 'material benefits' humanity draws from it. These benefits are related to the potential of biological diversity to act as a source for new food crops, types of renewable energy, industrial chemicals, raw materials, and medicines.[27] In this section, Norse and McManus seek to render explicit and explain the multiform role and contributions[28] of biodiversity to human society.

In addition to establishing its instrumental value, they also provide, in their words, a 'psychological and philosophical basis for preserving biological diversity'.[29] This part is closer to Moore's more traditional conservation concerns. Such basis can be drawn from the aesthetic and spiritual relation between humanity and nature. The authors stress that humans are both a part of nature, as well as apart; a 'transcendent species with unparalleled abilities'.[30] It is on this point that their problematization of humanity's impact is based: 'an ability to control the Earth that is unmatched. What our species does with this power depends on our definition of self.'[31] In this chapter, therefore, the advent of biodiversity is linked with a problematization of our individual and collective selves. The problematizing lens is turned towards society's conduct itself, and not just towards the naivety of conservation.

This problematization is structured around the binary between instrumental value (what the authors call utilitarianism) and existence or intrinsic value of species. The former approach is linked to the conception of species as resources, i.e., 'reserves of commodities' of indirect or direct economic value.[32] The authors seem to suggest that the aim of protecting biological diversity is instead based on the latter approach of intrinsic value, given its holistic emphasis on protecting every species. Such policies are considered akin to policies to protect human values, and thus 'extend the definition of the self to include nonhuman life'.[33] This is an early connection between the environment and notions of human rights. On the other hand, environmental law (or to be specific US federal acts related to environmental protection passed in the 1970s examined in the chapter in question), according to the authors, is driven by a mixture of both approaches, as utilitarianism alone is not sufficient in justifying their existence.[34] Where these two approaches (the 'new' biological diversity and the 'old' environmental protection/conservation enshrined in existing law) can meet is actually at the potential of biological diversity to become directly valuable in the future as a basis for conservation in the present.[35] This is recognition that aspects of biological diversity have unknown economic potential, even if their current instrumental value may be known to be limited.

The problematization subsequently moves to analyze the ways humanity reduces biological diversity.[36] These include land and sea use, transportation, pollution, forestry, agriculture, and what we call today 'invasive alien species'

28 Lambswool into synthetic

and the report calls by the term 'biological pollution'.[37] This is squarely faced at the societal and developmental choices, all under the spectre of a rapidly increasing human population. Of particular note is the realization that agriculture is both a beneficiary, drawing on biological diversity as a 'genetic reservoir,'[38] and a threat to biological diversity through its institution of intensive, industrialized monoculture, thereby reducing ecological diversity and genetic diversity in crops.[39]

In addition to mitigation of such human activities causing biodiversity decline, the authors also outline 'positive steps to preserve our biological heritage'.[40] This is the part where conservation enters the analysis. The chapter outlines three steps: the gene bank-zoo-botanical garden approach, the species approach, and the ecosystem approach. The first involves the conservation of endangered organisms and their genetic material in purpose-built facilities suited to the animals, plants, and other organisms being preserved. This form of *ex situ* conservation is considered a 'last ditch strategy for preserving biological diversity'.[41] The species approach echoes Moore's special measures for certain endangered or particularly valuable species selected for elevated protection. Thirdly, the ecosystem approach is similar to Moore's overarching aim, in that it seeks to intentionally preserve diversity rather than a component of it. It does so by seeking to delineate functioning and self-sustaining (with 'biologically meaningful, rather than political boundaries'[42]) ecosystems as the target of conservation. In contrast to Moore, however, minimal intervention in managing these nature reserves is envisaged, as long as the ecosystem is sufficiently large; 'because human ecological knowledge is incomplete, there is great virtue in letting nature take its course rather than intervening'.[43]

The chapter also assesses US conservation obligations stemming from international law, where black clouds are already observed in the reluctance of US states to acquiesce to international species conservation efforts due to in effect issues with sovereignty[44] and the absence of systematized programmes for the conservation of 'unique and representative' ecosystems.[45] The chapter closes with an economic metaphor emphasising biological diversity's instrumental/economic potential, following the *World Conservation Strategy*[46] published in the same year. It calls the 'earth's living resources' an 'incomparably rich national and global bank account', which, if managed properly, can be drawn upon 'in perpetuity, without depleting it'.[47]

The conception of biological diversity in the CEQ chapter incorporates tactical concerns of conservation into a comprehensive problematization of a profound loss affecting human society. By attempting to describe the problem(s) with life and nature as a whole, the authors were able to synthesize previously disparate environmental problems under a singular problematization of society's impact on nature. This was less about providing conservation with an overarching aim or unifying purpose, and more about daring to frame the issue more directly in terms of the relation between humanity and nature.

By expansion and synthesis, the chapter traversed into new territory that conservation only previously tiptoed around. It sought to explain and identify the value of biodiversity, as well as the impact of society on it, suggesting that 'everyone had some stake and responsibility in the preservation of biological diversity'.[48]

A mission in response to a crisis: conservation biology

During its emergence in the 1980s, the scientific field of conservation biology began to embrace biological diversity. Conservation biology was described as the 'application of science to conservation problems', aiming to 'provide principles and tools for preserving biological diversity'.[49] This project was based on the 'holistic assumption' that 'the proper objective of conservation is the protection and continuity of entire communities and ecosystems'.[50] Conservation biology was proposing 'a new stage in the application of science to conservation problems'.[51] Through the merger of ecology (as the science of studying ecosystems), biology, and conservation into a 'mission-oriented discipline comprising both pure and applied science',[52] conservation biology was seeking both a balance between theory and practice, as well as to 'crystalize' a 'new community of interest and concern'[53] for nature *as* biological diversity.

The field was thus developing a dual problematization, incorporating concerns regarding the unscientific regime of conservation practices, as well as its place and reception within society. Consequently, the subsequently developed programme was highly ambitious. Conservation biologists portrayed themselves as straddling the divide between academic field and environmental movement; they self-identified as 'alert and concerned citizens and scientists', who exercised their 'finely honed…scientific abilities in a large societal context'.[54] Conservation biologists aspired to influence 'the real worlds of institutions, government, and management'.[55] The apparatus of the state was in their sights. It was flatly stated that 'the ultimate test of conservation biology is the application of its theories in actual management situations'.[56]

Conservation biology identified two major obstacles to 'effective' conservation: the fact that conservation itself was not incorporating the findings of ecology and biology, and that it was still regarded as an activity standing in opposition to the economy.

Regarding the former issue, the identified issues echoed previous iterations that incorporated some aspect of biological diversity. It was thought conservation practice proceeded in a fragmented fashion and with a scattered focus, guided by vague concepts such as wilderness (especially in North America), the natural reserve, and endangered species. Fragments of natural landscapes were designated as protected areas based on their aesthetic valued as landmarks, political expediency (i.e., to be 'seen' as taking environmental action), or for economic reasons (i.e., it was land that could not be put to other productive

30 Lambswool into synthetic

use). Certain animals, mostly mammals possessing a certain aesthetic value and popular appeal for Western audiences, were stringently protected from indiscriminate hunting and general exploitation, while plants and other organisms of crucial importance to ecosystems were ignored.

Regarding the latter issue, conservation could still be cast in adversarial terms to the economy, easily depicted as a profoundly negative activity, 'stopping everything cold',[57] and dismissed as a radical ethical choice that prioritized the value of obscure organisms and 'invisible' ecosystems over human welfare. The 'rapprochement' between ecology and economy of sustainable development was still more than a decade away. This adversarial stance was deemed a problem for conservation biology, and conservation had to be able to compete on the economic front, as Norman Moore had recognized early on.

To compound this issue, however, the field 'did not, strictly speaking, include the subject of economics'.[58] Indeed, it could be argued that the negative, anti-economic attitude persevered into the label of conservation biology. Paul Ehrlich begins the last chapter of the 1980 edition of *Conservation Biology* with a call for 'dramatic changes in the socio-political, and especially, in the *economic systems* that dominate society today'.[59] The consequence of not effecting such dramatic change will be 'biotic Armageddon' and 'the disappearance of civilization as we know it'.[60] He adopts[61] Kenneth Boulding's characterization of the US economy as a 'cowboy' system, outlining through a case study what Boulding termed as the 'reckless, exploitative, romantic and violent behaviour'[62] of perpetual economic growth and expansion in search for more resources. Ehrlich decries the 'growth-manic economic system' as incompatible with conservation, in one of his proposed 'iron laws of conservation'.[63] This echoes earlier negative assessments expressed in David Ehrenfeld's work, where he identified the 'economics of perpetual expansion' as a source of the problem of the 'irreversible loss of diversity' in nature.[64] Ehrlich does not hesitate to use terms such as 'overdeveloped countries'.[65] Even though a main focus of attention is, of course, on population growth at the other end of the spectrum in terms of development, he accepts that 'economic growth rather than population growth *per se* is a potent anti-conservation force'.[66] Economic growth is actually deemed a 'major threat to Earth's life support systems'.[67] Ehrlich advocates for reduction in energy use and goes as far as lending support to Herman Daly's argument for a 'steady-state economy'.[68]

That is not to say that all biodiversity proponents and experts espoused such views regarding the relation between nature, society, and economy. Ehrlich himself appreciably toned down this anti-economic growth sentiment for his contribution to the bible of biodiversity six years later.[69] But there was clearly no shortage of criticisms of the economics of perpetual growth in emergent biodiversity thought. There was no shortage of problematizations of dominant economic ideas, based on their impact on biodiversity. Soule criticized the '*profane grail* of sustainable development' as the 'odd delusion of having your cake and eating it too',[70] even as late as 1995, after the link between biodiversity and sustainable development had been firmly established and internationally accepted in the CBD.

The abatement of the anti-economic sentiment allowed for the flourishing of a different problematization of biological diversity as a wasted resource. This was based on an analysis of the many economic benefits of plant and animal species that were developed around the same period.[71] These analyses served to cast species extinction as a wider economic, social, and political problem – by casting such species as necessary resources, whose extinction needs to be averted. Species, in addition to an object of scientific and taxonomic interest, as well as the subject of proto-ecological concern in the best tradition of Rachel Carson, were also becoming humanity's, 'our', natural resources. This eventually became the focus of conservation biology.[72] This problematization, therefore, framed the biodiversity crisis as a crisis related to nature conceived as capital squandered. As it was proven subsequently, this was only a step away from depicting biodiversity as genetic gold, i.e., as capital to be invested in.

These problematizations were distilled into some key propositions for a programme organized around biological diversity. These propositions, found in the 1980 edition[73] of *Conservation Biology* that is considered a landmark of the field, added some further core elements to the problematization. A crucial distinction, compared with previous treatments of biological diversity, was the geographical focus. As evidenced in part I of the volume, the tropical forests were considered the essential loci requiring conservation, due to the unknown amount of biological diversity hidden within them. This geographical focus would prove instrumental for the internationalization of the problematization of biodiversity. Furthermore, the protection of dispersed, small nature enclaves or reserves has no measurable effect on preserving the habitats of key species, especially if the designation of these areas relies on aesthetic and/or political reasons and is not supported by ecological science (and what subsequently became known as the 'ecosystem approach'). Echoing Moore once more, it was argued that nature reserves and protected areas should not be left in a state of 'benign neglect'; active monitoring and management are essential. *Ex situ* conservation (zoos, botanical gardens, seed banks, gene collections, etc.) was indeed a subsidiary measure. It will never be able to hold a significant amount of the world's biodiversity. Emphasis must be placed instead on *in situ* conservation, especially since knowledge of the precise number of species and the interaction between species, organisms, and ecosystems is constantly evolving and uncertain. A 'more expansive conservation paradigm'[74] was being formulated by conservation biology.

Finally, 'Man is an integral variable' of conservation, assuming roles as both a 'user' and a 'steward' of nature. Consequently, any discussion of conservation is incomplete without consideration of issues of exploitation/utilization.[75] Any new conservation paradigm will have to be integrated with some form of instrumental resource management. Irrespective of nuances and variations, and in the words of Michael Soule, 'the emphasis is on *our* natural *resources*'.[76]

32   Lambswool into synthetic

Conservation biology's own self-conception was that of an urgent movement emerging in response to a crisis of biodiversity loss, going beyond constituting a conservation paradigm, i.e., a set of aims and principles for the reform of conservation practice.[77] Armed with new ideas and with defective conservation practice in their sights, conservation biologists believed themselves to be forging ahead at the forefront: '[conservation biology's] relation to biology, particularly ecology, is analogous to that of surgery to physiology and war to political science.'[78] They were surgeons and fighters, people of decisive action, while others conversed. *They had indeed begun to marvel at their ability to manufacture awe.*

In effect, they were attempting to replicate Rachel Carson's *Silent Spring*, copying the discursive tactics of other environmental movements from the 1960s and 1970s. The criticism could be levelled then: such politics of biodiversity did not reflect the novelty, complexity, and nuance of the emerging concept; it was more of the same environmental politics. If all 'ecologically-inclined' sciences could present a united front regarding the general problem of biodiversity loss under the banner of biology, this would enhance the wider public's scientific literacy of environmental issues, this would raise pressure on the political sphere sufficiently to take concerted action to address this problem.

Delivering the Bible, and the popular contraction

The defining point for the popularization of the invention of biological diversity was the 'National Forum on BioDiversity' (*sic*), co-organized by the US National Research Council and the Smithsonian Institute. This multidisciplinary event was held in Washington, D.C., on 21–24 September 1986, attended by scientists, economists, conservationists, and policy makers. The forum conceived and disseminated the media-friendly contraction into 'biodiversity'. Its advocacy aimed to raise public awareness of a generalized environmental crisis linked to the disturbing phenomenon that had been identified by conservation biology as biodiversity loss. The contraction allowed for a neat packaging of the global environmental problem, and conservation biology's mission.

The forum proceedings were so influential that they were subsequently referred to as the 'Bible of Biodiversity'.[79] Chapters ranged from different methods for measuring and preserving elements and processes to be included under biodiversity,[80] to identifying the different values that may be attached to nature once conceived of as biodiversity,[81] to necessary policies that have to be adopted and solutions for the restoration of endangered biodiversity.[82] A significant number of papers presented at the forum focused on species diversity and the particular habitat of the rainforest, continuing on the geographical theme of conservation biology.[83] By capturing and presenting a mosaic of different environmental concerns, ecological traditions, conservation practices, and resource management ideas, merging ecological and biological theory with conservation concerns and practices, the volume was able to organize and popularize a particular unification of existing strands of environmental thought under the new synthesis and organizational schema provided by the field of conservation biology and particularly its now fully adopted master-concept of biodiversity.

The range of different approaches and understandings formulated one significant advantage of the concept: *familiarity* in addition to *innovation*. While biodiversity itself was presented as a novel term, the components and levels of its proposed reorganization of conservation and the natural world itself were familiar objects of research for ecologists, domains of practice for conservationists, and points of activism for environmentalists.

For example, a conservationist would focus on the extinction of species, reading biodiversity as a complex, but endangered, diagram of the 'production line' of evolution. An ecologist might focus on ecosystems, identifying diversity as an intrinsic property of natural communities, biotas, or the biosphere as a whole. An agricultural scientist would read biodiversity in the context of plant diversity required for maintaining and strengthening the world's food supply and security. An environmental economist would focus on the economic benefits that can be derived from the utilization of biodiversity, viewing biodiversity in an even more applied sense, as a global system of natural resources and services to be managed efficiently. An activist could concentrate on more localized campaigns for the protection of specific areas of aesthetic value or of specific endangered and 'charismatic' species. All of these perspectives were possible and can be found within the 'bible' of biodiversity.

Within the all-inclusive framework of biodiversity, all these ideas, emphases, and activities could be understood both separately, as well as together as a whole, exemplifying biodiversity's holistic 'character'[84] or 'sensibility'.[85] They may be referring to different issues, but they are all, in their own way, talking of biodiversity. The message was that 'biodiversity has to be thought of in a number of different ways,'[86] i.e., be 'a paradigm of nature conservation that *all* can rally behind'.[87]

The combined impact of the forum and the 'bible' that followed in 1988 represented an astute tactical achievement. The conceptual interdependence of biodiversity's components paralleled the functional interdependence of the planet's ecological processes and living things, thus mutually reinforcing the conceptual synthesis of the whole. Highly incontestable universal goods of diversity and interdependence became entrenched. The forum proceedings represented strong evidence that the problematization set out by conservation biology was becoming more sophisticated in its synthesis, encapsulating additional elements. In this way, this forum further consolidated conservation biology's objective of forming a community of interest and concern, around the biodiversity contraction:

> Conservation biologists have generated and disseminated the term biodiversity specifically to change the terrain of your mental map, reasoning

34   Lambswool into synthetic

that if you were to conceive of nature differently, you would view and value it differently[88].

By sharing their knowledge and marvel at the complexity of life on Earth as the natural output of the four billion-year evolutionary process and their increasing alarm over its continuing human-induced decline, the proponents of biodiversity were confident of getting people on board with the need for conservation.

The overall framing of the contraction of biodiversity was that of an 'extinction crisis'[89] of 'unprecedented urgency',[90] reinforcing conservation biology's position. Biodiversity knowledge had clearly demonstrated that species were disappearing and habitats degrading at an alarming rate. Surely the scientists more capable of understanding this unfolding disaster would be called upon to arrest its damaging course? The overall urgent tone of the writing implicitly and explicitly linked biodiversity with a rapidly escalating crisis,[91] further and above existing concerns over human exploitation of natural resources and pollution. To cement its mission, conservation biology had found a symbol that condensed its thought in the shape of biodiversity, which 'is a revolutionary term: its makers and promoters aim to foment radical changes on several fronts'.[92]

Unpleasant truths and global ambitions

Conservation biology was very much a project of Enlightenment. It had confidence in progress, both scientific and social. It regarded conservation and environmental protection in general as an activity to be governed by rational precepts that could be agreed upon with the assistance and reliance upon science. It regarded environmentalism as a progressive social movement, a benign continuation of the 1960s – Rachel Carson, the first Earth Day, the first pictures of Earth from space. It believed a narrative about humanity's rational progress.

Yet the proponents of biodiversity operated and advocated under a heavy shadow, clear in all their early writings and advocacy, including Moore. That shadow was human population, or rather the problematization of a global phenomenon called 'overpopulation', i.e., the 'unrestrained' growth of human population. This shadow created a darker 'timeline'; in place of the summer of hope (and love), a chilling autumn of societal collapse; in place of Woodstock, Altamont; in place of the celebration of science applied to the Space Race or the Green Revolution, a morbid fascination with the feral violence of the Manson Family; in place of an enlightened world, a post-apocalyptic one.

An expression of this darker view of the world, where biodiversity is threatened by overpopulation and the global consists of permanent competition over resources, can be found in the so-called 'bible of biodiversity', the proceedings of the national forum on biodiversity held at the Smithsonian in 1986. This view can specifically be found on Ehrlich's chapter on the causes and consequences of biodiversity loss,[93] as he was now abandoning his problematization of the economy and replacing it with a problematization of population. In the chapter, he calls for a focus of 'public attention' on 'more obscure and (to most people) unpleasant truths'.[94]

The first such truth is that biodiversity decline occurs primarily through habitat destruction brought about by the expansion of human population, and pointedly not 'direct human exploitation or malevolence'.[95] Another such truth is that the rationale for protecting biodiversity is the essential ecosystem services it provides to human society, i.e., the notion that it is *the essential* human life support system. 'The extirpation of populations and species of organisms exerts its primary impact on society through the impairment of ecosystem services.'[96] Additionally, the 'precipitous' decline of genetic diversity assumes greater importance, because it affects the ability of biodiversity to provide such benefits and services, acting as the precursor to the endangerment and extinction of the species altogether. 'Genetic diversity is part of the inheritance of (natural) capital that *Homo Sapiens* is rapidly squandering.'[97] Ehrlich's final proposition or truth is that conservation in protected areas and nature reserves will not suffice; 'a quasi-religious transformation leading to the appreciation of diversity for its own sake, apart from the obvious direct benefits to humanity, may be required to save other organisms and ourselves'.[98]

This seems relatively benign and rather prescient of subsequent and still contemporary thought regarding biodiversity. But a Malthusian imprint is lurking within, building over centuries:

> Above all, the growth of human population must be halted, since it is obvious that if the scale of human activities continues to increase for even a few more decades, the extinction of much of Earth's biota cannot be avoided.[99]

In the next few sentences, this is pushed even further: 'one can argue persuasively that the size of human population and the scale of human activities should be gradually *reduced* below present levels.'[100] The difficulty of such programmatic aims, and particularly the latter one, is recognized, since 'it means that the environmental impacts of the rich must be enormously curtailed to permit the poor a chance for reasonable development'.[101] Ehrlich had also underlined this in the past: 'the cornerstone of a rational programme should be a great reduction in the growth of throughput of energy and materials in the rich countries.'[102] If this were indeed the hard part; by inference, the contrast implied that the reduction of the size of human population would be easier.

The loss of biodiversity is attributed by Ehrlich to the loss of natural habitat, which was, in turn, an inevitable consequence of the expanding human population; all this ostensibly without a geographical qualifier. Nevertheless, so-called 'runaway' population growth[103] and 'uncontrolled' human encroachment on the natural environment through population growth are phenomena with a very particular geography. It is a symbol and a signal. It conjures images of the sprawling metropolises of the South, complete with surrounding slums, widespread pollution, and waste. Coupled with the rainforest and tropics focus of conservation biology and the rest of the 'biodiversity bible', the destruction of natural habitats due to the encroaching pressure of human population in practice is to be understood, by association, to occur predominantly in the poorer parts of the South, where the majority of 'unspoiled' and 'undeveloped' land, including the last areas of high biodiversity, still remain. The combined mental association is inescapable.

While nominally in a volume of biodiversity studies, Ehrlich's problematization expands beyond the concerns of conservationists and conservation biologists. What is at stake to prevent a catastrophe is 'a revolution in attitudes towards other people, population growth, the purpose of human life', and only after all these elements were enumerated did the 'the intrinsic value' of biodiversity make an appearance.[104] Of note, therefore, is this continuation of the expansion of the biodiversity problematization to take in wider concerns and foundational problems of government. In other words, biodiversity − the contraction − and its holistic, integrative programme became more ambitious. Arresting biodiversity decline was not a matter of governing human conduct towards nature, but of governing human conduct in general.

Through Ehrlich's work incorporating a neo-Malthusian trajectory, issues of resource scarcity and 'runaway' population growth came to prominence in the problematization of biodiversity. Combined with the emphases of conservation biology, the focus shifted, inexorably, like a large container ship, towards the Global South, the place where runaway population growth and biodiversity loss, through the destruction of the rainforest habitat, was occurring. Questions of conservation practices, species conservation, and the role of nature reserves were transformed into questions of human conduct (of a very particular segment of the global population) and the problems of the Global South. Such a problematization of biodiversity framed a series of biodiversity-related concerns that were venturing quite close to development concerns. In addition to conservation practices, society, and the economy, it was now the political economy of the Global South that was becoming governmentalized, i.e., becoming conceived as a problem of government within the context of biodiversity.

The issue remained, however, that conservation biology strictly speaking does not include the subject economics. By ever expanding the ambition of the biodiversity problematization, its proponents were venturing further and further into unknown areas, leading to embarrassing results. For example, the landmark 1980 edition of *Conservation Biology* includes a chapter on African wildlife resources, 'concerned with developing a profile of Africa's past in relation to the man–nature interface upon which a rational perspective for African wildlife in the future will be based'.[105] Notwithstanding any concerns about the continent's entire biodiversity constituting a valid object of scientific study, this supposed historical exploration apparently does not include any colonial-era imposed practices of land and resource management or overexploitation. 'Rhodesia' is praised for its well-organized game ranching operations, from which 'we have a great deal to learn'.[106] There are numerous pastoral portrayals of African life and analysis of the impact of local and traditional communities on biodiversity. The whole study is centred on ways to preserve the values of these natural resources, a project that takes priority over the absent concerns of African peoples. This is about 'our (*sic*) efforts to aid the African continent in rationally utilising her wildlife resources'.[107]

With the addition of the population problematization, the narrow scientific view clashed with the wider political and inescapably politicized problematization. The problem was no longer governing conservation, but governing society as a (global) whole, underpinned by the fear[108] of a world where the phenomenon of overpopulation unravels and overwhelms nature. Conservation biology was truly venturing into the real, *real* world of international politics, conceptually unprepared for globalising the problematization of biodiversity. Its lens was too narrow, constructed out of a combination of staggering naivety, wilful ignorance of history, and concerted avoidance of the political. Even when the 'needs of the developing nations of Africa' did enter the analysis, this is in relation to the future conservation of African wildlife.[109] And it is at that point in the analysis that the spectre of overpopulation makes its appearance once more.

Biodiversity discovered a competitive, bleak and dismal world, full of decline and limits, a few steps away from nuclear winter. The South was identified as the flashpoint of a global biodiversity crisis. The differentiated historical responsibilities of the North and the South were condensed into a thick haze of abstract, de-politicized, and collective responsibility. By obscuring questions of resource exploitation and distribution, the historical conditions for the concentration of both environmental degradation and widespread poverty in the South are consistently underplayed. Going forward, everyone became equally responsible for the degradation of the environment and biodiversity loss.[110] In this way, biodiversity became part of a global environmentalism that invoked scarcity without regard to equity.[111] By eradicating environmentalism's strongly-worded criticisms of fundamental economic tenets of capitalism, by absolving terms such as production, use, exploitation, or utilization of their 'dirty past', by focusing on the problems of the South, and by finally exiting the confines of North American-centric conservation concerns, the concept of biodiversity would be able to test its authority not only within the domestic policy agenda, but also internationally.

38 Lambswool into synthetic

The parameters of early biodiversity reason

The theme of these early prescriptive texts related to biological diversity is the construction of ever-widening problematizations. To a core problematization of conservation practices, a series of concentric circles of ever-widening problematizations were added on top by various proponents. Taken together, these problematizations, practices, and programmes outlined through the various texts discussed in this chapter offer a window into early biodiversity reason, that is to say, a form of governmental thought underlying efforts to address problems of biodiversity loss.

First, there was *biological diversity*, the problematization of unfocused and unscientific conservation practices emerging from within that same regime. Biological diversity thus emerged as an organising guide for conservation practice, aiming to bring about the shift away from the conception of nature conservation as essentially species conservation, and towards a more holistic and integrative approach. Biological diversity was a conservation paradigm, the symbol of a conservation programme that addressed issues of conservation practice.

Then, there was the contraction into *biodiversity*, a wider problematization pioneered by conservation biology. Biodiversity was far more ambitious; an integrative programme for unifying the disparities between environmental thought, conservation practice, and ecological sciences. The contraction was a composition, stitching together thought and practice into a new vision for the relation between humanity and nature. But this new vision remained embedded within a familiar milieu of existing traditions of ecological thought and conservation practice. In this way, biodiversity was at the same time something radically new, an invention that was also comfortably recognizable, a loud synthetic fabric made from lambswool.

Biodiversity reason is a rationality that is focused on making use of biodiversity. This use of biodiversity can be conceptual, political, or indeed economic, as it became in the context of genetic gold and more recently with the idea of ecosystem services. But even at its outset the core aspect of the programme was to use biodiversity to achieve certain ends; *to make productive use of it.*

Notes

1 Don DeLillo, *White Noise* (1984)
2 David Takacs, *The Idea of Biodiversity: Philosophies of Paradise* (The Johns Hopkins University Press 1996), 39.
3 Timothy J. Farnham, *Saving Nature's Legacy: Origins of The Idea of Biological Diversity* (Yale University Press 2007), 3.
4 N.W. Moore and J. O'G. Tatton, 'Organochlorine Insecticide Residues in the Eggs of Sea Birds' (1965) 207 *Nature* 42.
5 N.W. Moore, 'Experience with Pesticides and the Theory of Conservation' (1969) 1 *Biological Conservation* 201, 201.
6 Ibid.

7 Ibid, 202.
8 Ibid, 203.
9 Ibid.
10 Ibid.
11 Ibid, 204.
12 Ibid.
13 Ibid, 207.
14 A list of special categories is provided in ibid, 204–5.
15 Ibid, 205.
16 Ibid, 205.
17 Ibid, 206.
18 Ibid, 207.
19 Ibid.
20 Farnham (n.3), 205.
21 Elliot A. Norse and Roger E. McManus, 'Ecology and Living Resources: Biological Diversity', *Environmental Quality 1980: The Eleventh Annual Report of the Council on Environmental Quality* (Council on Environmental Quality 1980).
22 As established by the US National Environmental Policy Act (NEPA) of 1969. 83 Stat. 852.
23 Elliot A. Norse, 'A River that Flows to the Sea: The Marine Biological Diversity Movement' (1996) 9 *Oceanography* 5, 6.
24 Ibid.
25 Norse and McManus (n.21), 32.
26 Ibid.
27 Ibid, 32 *ff*.
28 Ibid, 32.
29 Ibid, 38.
30 Ibid.
31 Ibid.
32 Quoting David Ehrenfeld in this. Ibid, 39.
33 Ibid, 40.
34 Ibid.
35 'The discovery of the utilitarian values of the vast majority species will lie in the future, if humankind allows them in the future'. Ibid, 40.
36 Ibid, 42 *ff*.
37 Ibid, 61.
38 Ibid, 51.
39 Ibid, 48–50.
40 Ibid, 64.
41 Ibid, 65.
42 Ibid, 67.
43 Ibid, 69.
44 Ibid, 73.
45 Ibid.
46 This document is analyzed in Chapter 5 *infra*.
47 Norse and McManus (n.21), 74.
48 Farnham (n.3), 19.
49 Michael E. Soule, 'What is Conservation Biology?' (1985) 35 *Bioscience* 727, 727.
50 Ibid, 728.
51 Ibid, 727.
52 Michael E. Soule, 'Conservation and the "Real World"' in Michael E. Soule (ed), *Conservation Biology: the Science of Scarcity and Diversity* (Sinauer 1986), 1.

40 Lambswool into synthetic

53 Ibid, 2.
54 Michael E. Soule and Bruce A. Wilcox (eds), *Conservation Biology: An Evolutionary – Ecological Perspective* (Sinauer 1980) ix.
55 Soule, 'Conservation and the "Real World"' (n.52), 6.
56 Ibid, 2.
57 Soule and Wilcox (eds) (n.54), ix.
58 Ibid.
59 Paul Ehrlich, 'The Strategy of Conservation 1980–2000' in Michael E. Soule and Bruce A. Wilcox (eds), *Conservation Biology: An Evolutionary – Ecological Perspective* (Sinauer Associates 1980), 330.
60 Ibid.
61 Ibid, 331.
62 Kenneth E. Boulding, 'The Economics of the Coming Spaceship Earth' in Henry Jarrety (ed), *Environmental Quality in a Growing Economy* (The Johns Hopkins Press 1966) 9.
63 Ehrlich (n.1), 338.
64 David Ehrenfeld, *Biological Conservation* (Holt, Rinehart and Winston, Inc. 1970) , 207.
65 Ehrlich (n.59), 335.
66 Ibid, 339.
67 Ibid, 343.
68 Ibid, 343.
69 This shift is examined in Chapter 3 *infra*.
70 Emphasis added. Michael E. Soule, 'The Social Siege of Nature' in Michael E. Soule and Gary Lease (eds), *Reinventing Nature? Responses to Postmodern Deconstruction* (Island Press 1995) 159.
71 For the more influential examples see Norman Myers, *The Sinking Ark: A New Look at the Problem of Disappearing Species* (Pergamon 1979); Paul R. Ehrlich and Anne H. Ehrlich, *Extinction: The Causes and Consequences of The Disappearance of Species* (Gollancz 1981).
72 Soule, 'What is Conservation Biology?' (n.49), 728.
73 Soule and Wilcox (eds) (n.54).
74 Farnham (n.3), 14.
75 Soule and Wilcox (eds) (n.54).
76 Soule, 'What is Conservation Biology?' (n.49), 728.
77 Michael E. Soule, 'Tactics for a Constant Crisis' (1991) 253 *Science* 744.
78 Soule, 'What is Conservation Biology?' (n.49), 727.
79 Michael Flitner, 'Biodiversity: Of Local Commons and Global Commodities' in Michael Goldman (ed), *Privatizing Nature: Political Struggles for the Global Commons* (Pluto Press 1998).
80 Edward O. Wilson (ed), *BioDiversity* (National Academy Press 1988) Part 6.
81 Ibid, Parts 5 and 12.
82 Ibid, Parts 8 and10.
83 E.g., 'I concentrate on the tropical moist forests, because of all the major habitats, they are richest in species and because they are in greater danger' in ibid, 3.
84 Marjorie L. Reaka-Kudla and others (eds), *Biodiversity II: Understanding and Protecting Our Biological Resources* (Joseph Henry Press 1996).
85 Farnham (n.3), 15.
86 Reaka-Kudla and others (eds) (n.84), 7.
87 Emphasis added. Farnham (n.3), 15.
88 Takacs (n.2), 1.
89 E.g., see Paul Ehrlich, 'The Loss of Diversity: Causes and Consequences' in Edward O. Wilson (ed), *Biodiversity* (National Academy Press 1988).

90 Wilson (ed) (n.80), 3.
91 Farnham (n.3), 2.
92 Takacs (n.2), 309.
93 Ehrlich, 'The Loss of Diversity: Causes and Consequences' (n.89).
94 Ibid, 21.
95 Ibid.
96 Ibid, 24.
97 Ibid, 25.
98 Ibid, 22.
99 Ibid, 25.
100 Ibid, 26.
101 Ibid.
102 Paul R. Ehrlich and others, *Ecoscience: Population, Resources, Environment* (W.H. Freeman and Co 1972), 956.
103 Ehrlich, 'The Loss of Diversity: Causes and Consequences' (n.89), 22.
104 Ibid, 26.
105 Malcom Coe, 'African Wildlife Resources' in Michael E. Soule and Bruce A. Wilcox (eds), *Conservation Biology: An Evolutionary-Ecological Perspective* (Sinauer Associates 1980), 275.
106 Ibid, 291.
107 Ibid, 300.
108 Ehrlich has been particularly adept at the evocation of such fear. For example, he wrote in 1986 that the decline of biodiversity and ecosystem services will bring upon humanity 'consequences depressingly similar to those expected from a nuclear winter'. Ehrlich, 'The Loss of Diversity: Causes and Consequences,' (n.89), 25.
109 Coe (n.105), 298.
110 Frank Furedi, *Population and Development: A Critical Introduction* (Polity Press 1997).
111 David Harvey, *Justice, Nature and the Geography of Difference* (Blackwell Publishers 1996).

Chapter 3

The glare of international law and the grand bargain

Very soon everyone was using the shortened form – biodiversity – but with as yet little clear understanding of its meaning.[1]

This chapter examines a number of problematizations, related to biodiversity, but focused on the role of international law in this governmental project. It presents an eventual programme that sought to underline a particular treaty form as a solution to a – now global – problem of biodiversity loss. This form was that of a grand exchange, a 'grand bargain'[2] between the North and the South. Early on, a paper that served as the basis for the discussion of the implementation of the biodiversity convention's third goal of benefit sharing noted that:

> the Convention can be interpreted broadly as an instrument to promote the equitable exchange, on mutually agreed terms, of access to genetic resources and associated knowledge for finance, technology and participation in research.[3]

International precursors

An almost parallel timeline occurred during the decade of the 1980s, where similar concerns as those explored and expressed through conservation biology's and others' problematization of biodiversity and its generalized decline were being addressed at the international level. A number of international precursors to the CBD created the path towards this international treaty.

In the same year as Norse and McManus's first definition of biological diversity in their CEQ chapter (1980), the first edition of the World Conservation Strategy (WCS) was adopted at the international level,[4] as an 'intellectual framework and practical guide' for conservation practice around the globe. The WCS articulated what can be perceived as an antecedent to biodiversity conservation, termed 'living-resource conservation'. This WCS conservation method had three objectives: '(i) to maintain essential ecological processes and life-support systems, (ii) to preserve genetic diversity and (iii) to ensure the sustainable utilization of species and ecosystems'.[5]

Already in 1981, the Secretariat of the International Union for the Conservation of Nature (IUCN) was tasked with analyzing the 'technical, legal, economic and financial matters relating to the conservation, accessibility and use of (genetic) resources, with a view to providing the basis for an international arrangement'.[6] The work of Cyrile de Klemm, 'the real father of the Biodiversity Convention', according to some,[7] also prompted IUCN to begin the process of drafting a specialized biodiversity treaty, on the basis of a common heritage attributed to all plant genetic resources. The result of this process was the first draft treaty on the topic conceived at the international level. Put together in 1989 by IUCN, this set of draft articles was included in the negotiations and formed the textual basis of the eventual treaty. It contributed the basic conceptual structure for the treaty as a grand exchange, built on twin pillars of conservation/sustainable use and access. It proposed for the first time at international level a legal framework with the primary aim of securing a balanced exchange between conservation and access/use of biological and genetic resources.

While the notion that the North would be asked to fund conservation efforts in the South was only challenged in relation to the level of funding required, the underlying idea of this IUCN draft text was to sidestep that debate in its entirety. Instead, it suggested that by placing restrictions on free access to these resources a market would be created for them, where Northern states would pay for access, and not conservation. Conservation of these resources would be funded only by extension, by the economic value of the resources to be protected.[8]

This preparatory work by IUCN was not warmly received by either the Northern or the Southern negotiating blocs.[9] The notion of legally defining biodiversity as common heritage contradicted the principle of permanent sovereignty of natural resources that the South was seeking, while the constitution of an additional global environmental fund for a new conservation mega-treaty was rejected by Northern states already obliged to contribute to a sprawl of development and international aid funds, organizations, and efforts. As the first concerted response of classical international environmental law, the IUCN proposal appeared slow in its uptake of the realignments and the multiple trajectories of the concept of biodiversity

This draft text was formally brought to the CBD negotiating table in 1990,[10] and promptly and roundly dismissed as 'naive',[11] an obsolete blueprint for environmental protection. The draft treaty, called 'idealistic and mandatory in its approach' by the negotiators,[12] failed to include any precise mechanisms for realizing the economic potential of these resources and conceived a proposed biodiversity economy, centrally regulated by the global regime instituted by the proposed treaty; i.e., it went against the principle of national sovereignty over natural resources.

44 International law and the grand bargain

Between 8 and 19 June 1987, the UNEP's General Council converged for its fourteenth session in Nairobi. The Report of the World Commission on Environment and Development (Brundtland Report)[13] was presented and endorsed.[14] It is well known that the report systematized and ushered in the very influential concept of sustainable development. In chapter 6, titled 'Species and Ecosystems: Resources for Development', the Report – building on the WCS terminology of 'living resource conservation' – proposed alterations in the focus and aims of the development project by establishing a material link between environment and development. Environmental intervention should distance itself 'from scientific and conservationist terms' and towards the notion of the global environmental problems as 'a leading economic and resource concern'[15]. This shift was driven by the need to present a 'powerful economic rationale...to bolster the ethical, aesthetic and scientific cases for preserving them'[16] ('them' refers to species and their genetic code in the chapter). This economic rationale underpinning changes in environmental policy was specifically linked to the possibility of two new environmental markets, for 'genetic material' and for ecosystem services.

Economic rationale did not equate with market-based initiatives and private ownership. The Brundtland report also included a recommendation or 'priority proposal' to 'investigate the prospect of agreeing to a "Species Convention", similar in spirit and scope to the Law of the Sea Treaty...reflecting the principles of universal resources'.[17] The proposal further referenced the work IUCN was conducting in preparing such a convention, on the basis of the concept of common heritage. But there was an important qualification:

> Collective responsibility for the common heritage would not mean collective international rights to particular resources within nations. This approach need not interfere with concepts of national sovereignty. But it would mean that individual nations would no longer be left to rely on their own isolated efforts to protect species within their borders.[18]

The notion of a 'species convention' seems almost like an anachronism in the context of the neoliberal decade of the 1980s and concurrent US objections and continued non-ratification of UNCLOS. It was an argument in favour of additional international law and centralized control to a certain extent, despite the caveats attached to collective responsibility and common heritage; that instead of having separate treaties for different species (e.g., whales, migratory birds) or specific harmful practices or endangered habitats (e.g., trade in wild animals, freshwater resources) those instruments should all be centralized under a new unified 'law of nature'. The Brundtland report, therefore, did address concerns recognized within the biodiversity programme as developed by conservation biology, such as the perception of conservation as a negative activity, the changing political economy of the world, and others. But it achieved that goal without any reference to biodiversity.

The work of the WCED was also used as a basis for a UNEP report titled *Environmental Perspective for the Year 2000 and beyond*.[19] The latter, despite being more moderately phrased under the constraints of achieving consensus, still attracted a number of negative statements regarding its politics and its reach towards international economic and trade law. France perplexingly noted that 'it had difficulty associating environmental problems with political concepts in documents of United Nations bodies that were technical and economic in character',[20] outlining a seemingly clear distinction between messy global politics and environmental problematizations of a techno-scientific and economic manner. The United Kingdom 'shared the concerns of other delegations regarding the dangers of politicising UNEP'.[21] Germany noted that economic and political issues fall under the remit of other UN organs.[22] While these efforts were made to disconnect environmental interventions from political concerns, the representative of Mexico instead addressed the elephant in the room by highlighting 'the need to reform the international economic system so as to reduce inequality and the gap between developed and developing countries'.[23] While the rapprochement between economy and ecology via the idea of sustainable development was on the cusp of being widely accepted, the same could not be said about the equivalent rapprochement between ecology and global political economy.

At the conclusion of the meeting, the Brundtland report was adopted by UNEP and transmitted to the UNGA for its consideration and adoption.[24] The attached draft UNGA resolution unexpectedly makes some reference to some notion of a new problematization emerging, 'recalling' that the WCED had produced a report on the topic of the environment and something called the 'global problématique'.[25]

The glare of international law

Based on the Brundtland report's proposal for a new convention, the same 1987 UNEP General Council at Nairobi recognized that there is a 'need for adequate protection and preservation of biological diversity, because of both the intrinsic and economic value of the species concerned'.[26] Among the stream of decisions, this recognition can be found in a vaguely worded decision covering less than one page, with the title of 'rationalization of international conventions on biological diversity'.[27] It was adopted quietly by consensus, with no objections or additional comments by representatives. Yet echoes of the themes and tensions that would eventually characterize and dominate the whole global biodiversity regime can already be traced in this decision, as well as the combined output of this Nairobi meeting in 1987.

Following this recognition, UNEP decided to establish an *ad hoc* working group of experts 'to investigate the desirability and possible form of an umbrella convention to rationalize current activities in the field…and to address other areas that might fall under this convention'.[28] This event was in fact the

46 International law and the grand bargain

low-key 'debut' of biodiversity in international law, signalling its emergence as a problem of interest and concern to the field, but also overshadowed as it was from the very beginning by the high-profile Brundtland Report for which most delegates had gathered at Nairobi. However, this being the pre-contraction era, the object of negotiation was not even biodiversity *per se* yet:

> Because the phrase 'conservation of biological diversity' was so cumbersome a proposal to revert to the shorter, traditional concept of 'nature conservation' appealed to many delegates who had no deep knowledge of the subject. But this was fiercely attacked by the few scientific experts present who had a hard but eventually successful task in convincing the ignorant majority that biological diversity was the correct term. Very soon everyone was using the shortened form – biodiversity – but with as yet little clear understanding of its meaning.[29]

According to Fiona McConnell, who was present in these meetings as part of the UK delegation, biodiversity was clearly not yet a concept sufficiently internalized by the existing international network of diplomats, administrators, lawyers and economists, and related experts that regularly participated in such meetings and working groups. The precursors talked of nature conservation, living or natural or genetic resources. The community of interest and concern, the biodiversity 'movement', was just entering the halls of international law. Their influence was just meeting the glare of the international. The proposal itself for the establishment of the working group was formulated with significant input by the US delegation.[30]

This very first encounter between – then – biological diversity and international law led to the rejection of nature conservation and *de facto* imposition of biodiversity as the 'correct term' under the authority of science. This can be regarded as the opening salvo in the struggle over the control of the concept and resultant problematization in the international field. A new way of seeing nature was seeking formal legitimation from international law. The first battle over conceptual control of the problematization of biodiversity was fought during the very start of the negotiations and concerned the very naming itself (and little of substance) for what would eventually become the CBD.

Taking this 1987 UNEP decision together with the Brundtland report's 'priority proposal' could have meant envisioning a treaty that would represent some form of unified 'law of the sea' for land, a 'mega-treaty' to rationalize and unify disparate arrangements, principles, and customary law. The practice to be 'rationalized', with the inference that its legal irrationality constituted a problem, was still fragmented nature conservation, but now more specifically the representation of fragmented conservation priorities in the separate international legal regimes specializing in separate aspects of habitats, species, etc.

The mandate of the working group was clarified and divided – in the next UNEP governing council of 1989[31] – between the operational coordination of existing agreements and the adoption of a discrete framework convention, the latter of which became the biodiversity convention three years later. The new approach firmly linked biodiversity with sustainable development:

> For environmental, ethical, social, economic and technical reasons, the conservation and utilization of biological diversity is more than ever essential for...sustainable development and...human survival.[32]

This removed some of the confusion and further established biodiversity within the lexicon of international environmental law.

Also in 1989, and further to this UNEP decision, the UN general assembly formally placed biological diversity under the mandate of the planned UN Conference on Environment and Development of 1992.[33] Biodiversity had truly arrived at the international stage. In a highly symbolic manner, the life of biodiversity in the texts of international environmental law was intertwined and overshadowed by development almost from the outset. The first UNEP decision was indirectly overshadowed by the Brundtland report in 1987. By 1989, biodiversity was firmly part of the sustainable development agenda. But once biodiversity was fully exposed in the international stage, strange and unforeseen phenomena and events began to pile on and set the stage for the complete derailment of the American project of conservation biology.

Negotiating the grand bargain: biodiversity and development

The glare of the international law was particularly withering, given the manner of the 'discovery of the world' by scientists ensconced in the ivory tower of North American academia highlighted in the previous chapter. Biodiversity had started life as biological diversity, a problematization of unfocused and unscientific conservation practices, but entering a field formed out of discourses and practices of colonialism and imperialism, and development as the very attempt of the international in the 20th century to escape and overcome the legacies of injustice and inequality that dominated that particular plane. The discomfort expressed by some of the representatives in the discussion of the *Environmental Perspective* report highlighted in the previous section was precisely a manifestation of discomfort with the intimation that an environmental problematization was being widened to include a number of political concerns that were not strictly environmental in the technical-scientific-ecological sense of the biodiversity movement.

The conceptual toolkit of conservation biology, within which the contracted biodiversity was formed, was not equipped to address this different type of world. As the previous chapter highlighted, any perusal of the 'bible of biodiversity' or the various edited collections of essays concretizing and establishing the field can easily confirm this point. But what the biodiversity

48 International law and the grand bargain

problematization was bringing to the international level was an emphasis on the strange problem of 'overpopulation'. This emphasis, exemplified by Ehrlich's contributions to biodiversity texts, had two political effects at the juncture when biodiversity met the glare of international law. First, it was interpreted as an attempt to shift political questions of historical responsibility for environmental problems from the North to the South. Second, this renewed interest in the Global South created the opportunity for a contested *quid pro quo*, an exchange, a grand bargain that would underpin agreement on what eventually became the CBD.

In terms of shifting responsibility, the narrative of the Northern biodiversity movement appeared to signal that the Global South is responsible for biodiversity loss due to its perceived overpopulation, but everyone should be responsible going forward, as long as proper biodiversity conservation and management methods are adopted, given that the vast majority of biodiversity reserves are also located in the Global South. This problematization, therefore, framed the South as an object of government that constituted both the source and the solution to the global biodiversity crisis.

This perception was contested[34] by the notion of ecological debt[35] that has the effect of 'turning overpopulation on its head'.[36] Aiming to switch focus to the conditions of unjust and unequal exchange that underpin the global political economy, it argues that a macro-'loan' of natural resources was used to drive unprecedented economic growth in the North via various combinations of the vehicles of capitalism, imperialism, colonialism, and, in the 20th century, developmentalism. This is a type of debt that has never been – and was never meant to be – paid back.

In place of overpopulation, overconsumption and the pursuit of unrestrained economic growth at all costs are installed as the primary causes of environmental problems, such as the biodiversity loss in question. Overexploitation replaces overpopulation on the pedestal as the primary cause of environmental degradation. Increased resource extraction and biodiversity exploitation was driven by the former in the now developed parts of the world and not the latter, occurring in the so-called 'developing' parts.

While the South accepted that it held the key to biodiversity's salvation, it refused to bear the imposed responsibility for its degradation. The South could counter-claim: the North is responsible for biodiversity loss due to overexploitation, but everyone's responsible going forward, as long as the North adopts proper restitution methods for the large debt accrued; for example, through a significant transfer of funds in order to implement much needed biodiversity conservation, as well as other forms of transfer of technological and governmental capacity. The operation and effect of this Southern counter-claim is evident in the fact that large parts of the negotiations for the CBD were consumed by discussions regarding the substantial funding arrangements required for the vast conservation undertakings implied by such a large-scale endeavour.[37]

International law and the grand bargain 49

It was not a step too far to construe biodiversity as an economic opportunity for the Global South:

> Their possession of the mainly untapped resource potential of species biodiversity within their territories presents them with an unrivalled opportunity to finally to gain what may euphemistically be called lost development ground...Access to these resources should therefore be jealously guarded, especially from would be competitors who lack such species biodiversity within their own jurisdictions.[38]

In the above one can observe the effect of international precursors highlighted in the first section of this chapter, in terms of conceiving of the biodiversity problematization as related not generally to conservation practices, but specifically on the instrumental value of biodiversity, of making use of biodiversity as a resource to achieve particular political and economic goals, in this case related to sustainable development. This commodification of biodiversity was also deplored on environmental and social justice grounds.[39] As a correlation of this problematization, the idea of a trade-off between conservation and development was often presented as the underlying rationale of the biodiversity regime.[40]

Under such a frame, securing control over this 'untapped resource potential' inevitably assumed primary importance. This was achieved through the recognition of the principle of permanent sovereignty over natural resources in Article 4 of the CBD. In effect, the Global South would be seeking to:

> Receive the maximum possible returns for the use of the plant and animal species extracts that are initially found within their territory...which would entail a complete restructuring of the present world market system for pricing raw materials used in industrial production.[41]

Such a negotiating stance was more reminiscent of debates surrounding the principles of self-determination and permanent sovereignty over natural resources and the NIEO, rather than the environmental concern that prompted the invention of biodiversity in the first place. From such a starting point, any international interest in biodiversity can be interpreted as another form of interventionism to be resisted.[42] Biodiversity was being transplanted into a context of North–South relations.[43] In such a context, the 'bible of biodiversity' had little to offer in this area of political economy; rainforest essentialism and controversial fetishism of 'runaway population growth' were not going to cut it. Biodiversity was an opportunity for the developed world to pay, to settle its ecological debt. A new political economy began to swirl around biodiversity.

Therefore, Ehrlich's particular view of the world, as reflected and incorporated within the biodiversity problematization, provided the basis for an international negotiation divided across North–South lines, as well as sufficient

50 International law and the grand bargain

leverage for both sides at the negotiating table. The North wanted to conserve biodiversity, but also wanted access to the genetic resources contained therein. The South wanted access to funding and technology. A notional grand balance was, therefore, being sought in biodiversity thought, between overexploitation in the North and overpopulation in the South. This search set the stage for a grand bargain, between the South, possessing genetic resources to which the North requires access to further develop its biotechnology industry, and the North, possessing the scientific, technical, and financial means that the South requires for sustainable development.[44] In this way, and without prejudice as to whether this bargain 'worked' in reality, the CBD could be conceived as a mechanism of exchange, as suggested in the beginning of this chapter.

Conservation biology and sociobiology lacked the conceptual apparatus to provide an answer to the political question of biodiversity, which was now a question of economic development as much as a problem of conservation practices. The starting concern was finding ways to fund costly conservation of the significant biodiversity reserves required, yet it morphed into a much broader political economic question regarding achieving the development of the Global South. The initial biodiversity movement had lost control of its buzzword.

When biodiversity became internationalized, it came face to face with a whole different field of the political economy of development. For conservation biology and the early proponents and members of the biodiversity movement, the Global South was the *object* of biodiversity-related problematizations, but never the subject, the author capable of formulating its own version of biodiversity as a problem of government. The elevation of biodiversity into the international plane and the prospect of negotiating a major convention enabled the maturation of this process.

An American project derailed: technology transfer as part of the grand bargain

The first proposal for a biodiversity treaty in 1987 was organized around the objective of the rationalization of the fragmented mosaic of existing conservation treaties. Alterations and reconfigurations of this objective occurred between 1987 and the signing of the treaty in 1992. Sustainable development structured new forms of environmentalism that co-existed with developmentalism, leading to a biodiversity reason that was quite different. The Global South engaged and contested the constructed truths of the biodiversity problematization. Biodiversity was coming face to face with a global political economy of demands and interests that went far beyond the environmental sphere. For some in the North, as already discussed above, the project of achieving agreement on a new biodiversity conservation treaty had clearly got out of hand. There was too much politics, not enough technical and managerial problem-solving, not enough problematization of conservation, and quite a lot of problematization of the economy.

The apparent final straw for the US, the original driver of the whole initiative for a biodiversity treaty as a rationalizing conservation instrument, came with the inclusion of biotechnology in the biodiversity frame. In 1989, it was proposed that in the working group for the negotiation of the biodiversity treaty:

> [t]he full implications of the new biotechnologies should be taken into account in any international legal instrument on the conservation of the biological diversity of the planet.[45]

Biotechnology was indeed included in the treaty text. To the intense disappointment of US biotechnology companies,[46] it was included in the technology transfer provisions of the treaty text.[47] Thus, technology transfer, one of the 'essential elements for the attainment of the Convention',[48] was also historically acknowledged as one of the main reasons for the US continued rejection of the treaty.[49] In particular, the requirement that any technology transfer to the developing world must be 'under fair and most favourable terms, including on concessional and preferential terms where mutually agreed',[50] i.e., potentially below market prices, proved a 'bridge too far'.[51] It was interpreted with suspicion as 'code for forced transfer of technology and which relieves developing countries of the burden of protecting the intellectual property rights of US biotechnology companies'.[52]

Raising further concerns was the grammar of Article 15 relating to benefit-sharing, and in particular the following wording:

> with the aim of sharing in a fair and equitable way the results of research and development and the benefits arising from the commercial and other utilization of genetic resources with the Contracting Party providing such resources.[53]

Research and development is distinguished from utilization, which, in turn, produces a second – undefined – distinction between results (of R&D) and benefits (of commercial activity). This was depicted by the US as a 'ploy' by the Global South to interfere and circumvent the emerging intellectual property regime being negotiated at the WTO by forcing the transfer of patented biotechnology; i.e., the 'results' of research and development.[54] Secondly, the open-ended nature of the term 'other utilization' of genetic resources also created confusion as to what kind of activities would create an obligation for benefit-sharing, fuelling additional fears over forced transfers of technology and compulsory licensing regimes.

The biotechnology industry was thus concerned that the treaty's non-existent treatment of intellectual property rights (for example, the lack of mandate

52 International law and the grand bargain

for a *sui generis* patent system) would allow the copying of inventions either through compulsory licensing systems or plain absence of legal protection. Such a possibility plainly contradicted the concurrent effort of the US administration to achieve a World Trade Organization (WTO) and to push for expansive and strictly enforced intellectual property regimes. The latter effort was concluded in 1995, and, by that time, the biodiversity convention had already been rejected by the US.[55]

Other measures were also not warmly received. The proposed joint ventures in the South constituted 'anathema to some members of that industry who fear that those countries would expropriate the fruits of such research, just as some Middle East oil states expropriated American oil wells'.[56] Additional concerns over the control (voting rights) of the proposed financial mechanism were also expressed in the official US declaration. The declaration finally lamented a treaty text that does not 'reflect well on the international treaty-making process in the environmental field'. There was too much politics within the grand bargain. The global problematization of biodiversity had expanded way beyond its original remit as a programme of rationalization of conservation activities.

These shifts in treaty construction suggest that the primary proponent, at state level, of the problematization of biodiversity had no firm control over it once it came into contact with the international level's own problematizations. As a result, it was ultimately disappointed and frustrated with the directions that other interlocutors were taking the problematization towards, as well as the final result in terms of a treaty text. The dispute was about the 'international law-making process' or rather what is the proper content (and form) of such a process. The US clearly regarded, and, based on its continued reluctance to accept the CBD, still regards, biotechnology and intellectual property rights as something that should not be considered part of biodiversity's problematizations or perhaps international environmental law in general. Whatever the influence of biodiversity's established community of interest and concern and movement within the confines of a state, the US withdrawal from the process of formulating a global biodiversity regime confirms the different conditions of the international.

A major international treaty on biodiversity was agreed and signed only five years after the publication of the 'bible of biodiversity' and seven years after the forum created the biodiversity contraction in the first place. The US was also the academic home of conservation biology and the majority of biodiversity proponents.[57] The US thus can be said to have nurtured biodiversity, only to abandon it when the problem of biodiversity loss assumed an international legal form. The US maintains its rejection to this day, although it still participates in an observer capacity.

The 'Like-Minded Group of Mega Diverse Countries'

The 'Like-Minded Group of Mega Diverse Countries' is a coalition of Southern states, 'holders' – their own term – of nearly 70% of the planet's biodiversity, that was very active at the turn of the 21st century. The core consisted of Brazil, China, Colombia, Costa Rica, India, Indonesia, Kenya, Philippines, Mexico, Peru, South Africa, and Venezuela before expanding to include more Southern states. The group's sole major output was the 2002 Cancun Declaration, which fully embraced the idea of biodiversity's multiple values:

> The resources of biological diversity and the environmental services that depend on them have an immense strategic, economic and social value, and offer development opportunities to our populations and to the international community.[58]

The declaration has an obvious lineage to the New International Economic Order, especially in the notion of a new 'general ethic of equity'. In contrast to the past, however, this new ethic is not presented as a new general principle or customary practice of international law, but as a diffuse guide for action for both state and non-state actors.

Under this new ethic, conservation and sustainable use are ensured by 'responsible attitudes', with no reference to states in particular. This is then paired with a new economy 'associated with the use of biological diversity, genetic resources and biotechnology'. The 'urgent need' outlined is not related in any way to any perceived environmental or biodiversity crisis, but 'to develop human resources, institutional capabilities, as well as an appropriate legal framework and public policies to enable our countries to take an *active part* in the new economy'.[59] In another subtle twist of the standard expectations of international environmental law, concern is further expressed over the limitations of international instruments in terms of protecting – not biodiversity itself – but the 'legitimate interests of the countries of origin of biodiversity'. In the decisions of the declaration, the Group was committing to:

> Ensure that the goods, services and benefits arising from the conservation and sustainable use…are utilized for the development of *our peoples*, seeking among other objectives to improve upon food safety, overcome health problems that affect us, and preserve our cultural integrity.[60]

The Cancun Declaration represents a good example of the reversal that occurred with the internationalization of biodiversity and its transformation into genetic gold. Biodiversity (and its protection) was not the endpoint, but a means to obtain something. Biodiversity was a development opportunity. The declaration was a forceful statement of belief in the idea of biodiversity as a valuable resource and of intent to utilize this realization in the pursuit of their self-defined socioeconomic trajectories, their articulation of development models. This was an expansion of a narrower and more localized INBio model. It appeared that, at least at the macro level of certain Southern states, the problematization of biodiversity was being enthusiastically embraced.

The irresponsible state and the international community

Turning back to the jurisdictional scope of the convention, we can observe in some quarters a lament for the fact that the principle of permanent sovereignty over natural resources has survived into the text of the treaty.[61] Francesco Francioni suggests, employing implicit scare quotes, that this demonstrates that the CBD 'remained attached to the traditional "Westphalian" model of international law as legal order created by states' and 'endorsed the entrenched idea that states are allowed to "privatize" parts of the physical space of the planet under the mantle of "territorial sovereignty"', which 'runs counter to the cosmopolitan of "common heritage" of biological resources'.[62] Patricia Birnie, Michael Bowman, and Catherine Redgwell, in their celebrated and foundational textbook of international environmental law, conceive and present the convention as a series of obligations that constrain the exercise of national sovereignty.[63] The recognition in the preamble that the conservation of biodiversity constitutes a common concern of humanity is emphasized as a check on sovereignty; as is the repeated contention that biodiversity forms 'a *de facto* global commons, similar to atmospheric resources, since the biosphere interconnects ecosystems and overrides national boundaries'.[64]

There is a *need* to conceive biodiversity as a global problem via the assistance of legal doctrines related to the commons. There is a *belief* that biodiversity loss should transcend human borders, so that international environmental law can rise and meet this problem square on. This is to justify the role, legitimacy, and authority of international environmental law as the appropriate governmental response and part of an international solution. The state is weak and irresponsible; it needs the international community to keep it on the proverbial environmental 'straight and narrow'. International environmental law, as a form of higher law, is needed to constrain and guide their actions.

There is, thus, the argument that state parties to the CBD assume certain responsibilities towards biodiversity as quasi-representatives of the will of the international community understood as a collective humanity, not just a collective of states.[65] This relies on a reading of the inclusion of the notion of common concern of humanity in the preamble of the CBD, in conjunction with its inclusion in other environmental agreements, such as the UNFCC. This argument seeks to establish a balance between sovereign control over natural resources and the presumed interests of an international community as the representative of humanity by reformulating the precise nature of state sovereignty, from seemingly unrestrained right to exploit such resources to something that has been called custodial sovereignty or, taking it further, a *public trusteeship model*.[66]

The latter is posited as the proper role of state sovereignty over natural resources: 'the message is simple: The sovereign rights of nation states over certain environmental resources are not proprietary, but fiduciary'.[67] This, of

International law and the grand bargain 55

course, is designed to set the stage for the emergence of the argument that this form of resource trusteeship is based on widely established customary law.[68] The beneficiary of the trust appears to be humanity as a whole, and the state is the actor that has to act in line with fiduciary obligations and the terms of a trust managed, in effect, by international environmental law.

This is yet a different way to problematize state sovereignty as the source of the problem of biodiversity loss. The difference is that this problematization appears to focus on the internal aspects of sovereignty, whereas the global problematization outlined in the previous section appears to focus on the external aspects, meaning the relation between the state and the international community. Restraint is placed on the exercise of sovereignty, so as the state would not think of itself as analogous to an owner of such natural resources. From this argument, therefore, we have to infer a very negative conception of ownership; a belief that an owner of resources will exploit them without limit, to the detriment of all. This is a problematization of a particular mentality, or subjectivity.

This should not have been surprising as, for example, the Netherlands Committee of the IUCN was still conceiving, in 1991, the whole Rio UNCED as 'a major step towards a global regime of the biosphere, which is both effective and fair'.[69] This conception was based on a firm belief in environmental protection as a common good, going as far as positioning law against the market:

> It is the firm conviction of the Netherlands committee that the new system of world governance should be firmly rooted in law. The free market, successful as it may be in providing consumers with a certain range of goods and services, can never manage a collective good by its own. The biosphere is probably the most collective of all collective goods.[70]

This spirit of promoting the rule of law as opposed to the rule of the market identified law with the law of the sovereign state. At its heart, it was another problematization of international law; an argument for more state regulation, promoting *in situ* conservation backed by international publicly administered funding. It even attributed to biodiversity the legal status of common heritage of humankind, removing it from national jurisdiction. The few concessions given to market rationality, such as the idea of states paying for access instead of conservation, were not enough to divert that draft text from proceeding down the same path of a largely 'command-and-control' approach. Since biodiversity was legally considered common heritage under this draft treaty, states would have to pay into a global fund for managing biodiversity.

The draft IUCN articles attempted to construct an international regime as a continuation or culmination of existing legal forms and mechanisms, envisaging the role of the biodiversity convention as a copy of existing treaties on a grander scale. International law and the biodiversity field were thus not an easy

56 International law and the grand bargain

match. They did not instantly conceive of the problem of biodiversity loss in a compatible way – even though they all talked about biodiversity.

The echoes of this mega-treaty that would never come to pass long endured in environmental law even after the entry into force of a different biodiversity convention. In 1995, Alan Boyle was noting that the agreed convention 'represents an attempt...to internationalize, in a more comprehensive and inclusive way, the conservation and sustainable use of nature',[71] lamenting how previous agreements 'fall short of establishing a comprehensive global regime for the protection of nature, and largely leave untouched resources located wholly within a state's own national boundaries'.[72] In a similar vein, Timothy Swanson argued as late as 1999 that the biodiversity convention was supposed to achieve 'the centralized management of global land use planning',[73] and that it exists 'as a monument along the pathway of increasingly active intervention in the process of national development planning and decision-making'.[74] Such assessments seem more apt to the rationalizing treaty that never materialized, rather than the actual treaty agreed, signed, and entered into force. They are, however, a sign that years after its signing the biodiversity convention remained opened to –often contentious – interpretation. It was still unclear what the problematization, practices, and programmes – the biodiversity reason – was.

This grand bargain materialized because even more elements and problematizations were added to biodiversity during the effort to transform it to a global problematization to which international law should respond.

The conservation burden – early global biodiversity reason

This chapter focused on the genealogy of the problem of devising the 'correct' international legal framework (and by extension regional, transnational, national, and local regulatory environment) for this object of government called biodiversity, which is almost like another name for nature, but consists of a number of different natural resources. It was about finding the right balance between conserving and using these resources, a question that became inveigled with the start with questions of sustainable development, leading to a subsequent question of a – second – balance between the North and the South.

Under this context of pursuing multiple balances, treaty negotiations were dominated by the conception of biodiversity conservation as a burden. This is an activity that needs to be undertaken for the good of biodiversity itself and thus the international community – however defined – yet remains at the very least in an economic sense a burden. This taps into the tradition of environmental thought explored in Chapter 4, whereby the perception of conservation as a negative activity is problematized. Sustainability and biodiversity itself, or rather the interplay between the two, was considered a solution for a time, as reflected in the CBD. In more recent years, ecosystem services played this role of a solution to the problem of conservation.

With the aid of international law, the problematization suggests a global, geopolitical, reorientation of conservation, from a political and financial burden to biodiversity as a programme of opportunity. This is linked to overcoming an anti-economic sentiment in environmental thought, which biodiversity, along with sustainable development which is not the sole originator of this shift contrary to existing understandings in the literature, appear to have greatly facilitated. The notion that the South possessed biodiversity and the North the financial resources and the willingness to pay for access and conservation underpinned a compromise of a North–South grand bargain. This became an essential guiding idea for the negotiation and early operation of the CBD.

The genealogy so far outlines the complexity and contingency of the use of biodiversity in its early emergence, as well as after its encounter with international law. Within the same time period, the problematization of something first called 'biological diversity' and then contracted to 'biodiversity' was concurrently understood and applied in different ways, by different disciplines and in different quarters of the world. Biodiversity was described as 'a metaphorical magnate that currently galvanizes the conservation, scientific and funding communities'.[75] Within a different schema of geopolitical exchange, a North–South 'grand bargain',[76] biodiversity was defined as a genetic resource held by Southern states and sought by Northern states. The LLMC group stressed that:

> The resources of biological diversity and the environmental services that depend on them have an immense strategic, economic and social value, and offer development opportunities to our populations and to the international community.[77]

Notes

1 Fiona McConnell, *The Biodiversity Convention: A Negotiating History* (Kluwer Law International 1996), 5.
2 Kerry ten Kate and Sarah A Laird, 'Biodiversity and Business: Coming to Terms with the "Grand Bargain"' (2000) 76 *International Affairs* 241; Walter V. Reid and others, *Biodiversity Prospecting: Using Genetic Resources for Sustainable Development* (World Resources Institute, USA 1993).
3 UNEP/CBD/COP/3/Inf. 53 (1996).
4 IUCN and others, *World Conservation Strategy: Living Resource Conservation for Sustainable Development*, 1980).
5 Ibid. This set of objectives is closer to the CBD than the subsequent work of American biologists.
6 IUCN General Assembly resolution 15/10 (1981).
7 Peter H. Sand, 'The Concept of Public Trusteeship in the Transboundary Governance of Biodiversity' in Louis J. Kotzé and Thilo Marauhn (eds), *The Transboundary Governance of Biodiversity* (Brill 2014), 34.
8 John H. Barton, 'Biodiversity at Rio' (1992) 42 *Bioscience* 773.
9 Sand (n.7), 35–37.
10 In the First Meeting of the ad hoc Group of Legal and Technical Experts, Nairobi, November 1990.

58 International law and the grand bargain

11 McConnell (n.1), 26–27.
12 Ibid, 26.
13 UN Doc A/42/427.
14 UNEP/GC/Decision 14/14 (1987).
15 UN Doc A/42/427, 162.
16 UN Doc A/42/427, 149.
17 UN Doc A/42/427, 163.
18 Ibid.
19 UNEP/GC Decision 14/13 (17 June 1987). This report in its entirety is included as Annex II to UNGA A/42/25 (1987) *UNEP Report of the Governing Council on the Work of its Fourteenth Session 8–19 June 1987*, 96–129.
20 Ibid, 14.
21 Ibid, 15.
22 Ibid.
23 Ibid, 14.
24 UNEP/GC Decision 14/14 (17 June 1987).
25 UNGA A/42/25 (1987). 61. The text remained the same in the adoption of the Brundtland report by the UNGA, via UNGA A/RES/42/187 (1987).
26 UNEP/GC/Decision 14/26 (1987).
27 Ibid.
28 Ibid.
29 McConnell (n.1), 5.
30 The draft proposal for what became decision 14/26 was formally tabled by the representatives of Australia, Canada, the Netherlands, and the United States, in consultation with the IUCN.
31 UNEP/GC Decision 15/34 (1989).
32 UNEP/GC Decision 15/34, (1989), Preamble.
33 UNGA/RES/44/228 (1989).
34 Although the South is argued to have engaged with international environmental fora in more constructive terms in recent years. See Adil Najam, 'Developing Countries and Global Environmental Governance: From Contestation to Participation to Engagement' (2005) 5 *International Environmental Agreements* 303.
35 See generally Juan Martínez Alier, *The Environmentalism of the Poor: A Study of Ecological Conflicts and Valuation* (Edward Elgar Publishing 2002), 213 ff.
36 John Barry, *Environment and Social Theory* (2nd edn, Routledge 2007) 233.
37 On the repetition of this theme during the negotiations see generally McConnell.
38 R. Jayakumar Nayar and David Mohan Ong, 'Developing Countries, "Development" and the Conservation of Biological Diversity' in Catherine Redgwell and Michael Bowman (eds), *International Law and the Conservation of Biological Diversity* (Kluwer Law International 1995) 237.
39 For some critiques see indicatively Kathleen McAfee, 'Selling Nature to Save it? Biodiversity and Green Developmentalism' (1999) 17 *Environment and Planning D: Society and Space* 133; Chapter 6 in Ramachandra Guha and J. Martinez-Alier, *Varieties of Environmentalism: Essays North and South* (Earthscan 1997).
40 See Alan E. Boyle, 'The Rio Convention on Biological Diversity' in Catherine Redgwell and Michael Bowman (eds), *International Law and the Conservation of Biological Diversity* (Kluwer Law International 1995) 38; Clare Shine and Palitha T.B. Kohona, 'The Convention on Biological Diversity: Bridging the Gap Between Conservation and Development' (1992) 1 *Review of European Community and International Environmental Law* 278; Catherine Tinker, 'A "New Breed" of Treaty: The United Nations Convention on Biological Diversity' (1995) 13 *Pace Envtl L Rev* 191; and Chapters 3 and 4 in this volume.

International law and the grand bargain 59

41 Nayar and Ong, 237.
42 Ibid, 236–41.
43 Ibid, 237.
44 Timothy Swanson, 'The Reliance of Northern Economies on Southern Biodiversity: Biodiversity as Information' (1996) 17 *Ecological Economics* 1.
45 UNEP/GC Decision 15/34, Nairobi, 1989, Preamble.
46 Michael D. Jr Coughlin, 'Using the Merck-INBio Agreement to Clarify the Convention on Biological Diversity' (1993) 31 *Colum J Transnat'l L* 337.
47 CBD, Art. 16.
48 CBD, Art. 16.1.
49 See US Declaration on the CBD, 31 ILM 848 (1992). Also Klaus Bosselman, 'Poverty Alleviation and Environmental Sustainability through Improved Regimes of Technology Transfer' (2006) 2 *Law, Environment and Development Journal* 19.
50 CBD, Art. 16(2).
51 For more information on the problems with the interpretation of the CBD's technology transfer provisions, see Biswajit Dhar, 'The Convention on Biological Diversity and the TRIPS Agreement: Compatibility or Conflict?' in Cristophe Bellman and others (eds), *Trading in Knowledge: Development Perspectives on TRIP, Trade and Sustainability* (Earthscan 2003).
52 Coughlin (n.46), 346.
53 CBD, Art. 15.7
54 Coughlin (n.46), 348.
55 See the US declaration made at the UNEP Nairobi Conference for the Adoption of the Agreed Text of the Convention on Biological Diversity, 22 May 1992, (1992) 31 ILM 848.
56 Coughlin (n.46), 346.
57 As evidenced in Chapter 2 *supra*.
58 Cancun Declaration of Like-Minded Mega Diverse Countries (18 February 2002).
59 Emphasis added. Ibid.
60 Emphasis added. See n.17 above.
61 CBD, Art. 3.
62 Francesco Francioni, 'Foreword' in Elisa Morgera and others (eds), *Unraveling the Nagoya Protocol: A Commentary on the Nagoya Protocol on Access and Benefit-Sharing to the Convention on Biological Diversity* (Brill 2015), XIII.
63 Patricia Birnie and others, *International Law and the Environment* (3rd edn, Oxford University Press 2009), 621 ff.
64 Aline Jaeckel, 'Intellectual Property Rights and the Conservation of Plant Biodiversity as a Common Concern of Humankind' (2013) 2 *TEL* 167, 168.
65 Ibid, 173.
66 Ibid; Werner Scholtz, 'Custodial Sovereignty: Reconciling Sovereignty and Global Environmental Challenges amongst the Vestiges of Colonialism' (2008) 55 *Netherlands International Law Review* 323.
67 Peter H. Sand, 'Sovereignty Bounded: Public Trusteeship for Common Pool Resources?' (2004) 4 *Global Environmental Politics* 47, 48.
68 Jaeckel (n.64), 174.
69 Simone Bilderbeek (ed), *Biodiversity and International Law: The Effectiveness of International Environmental Law* (IOS Press 1992), Preface.
70 Ibid.
71 Boyle (n.41), 33.
72 Ibid, 33.
73 Timothy Swanson, 'Why is There a Biodiversity Convention? The International Interest in Centralized Development Planning' (1999) 75 *International Affairs* 307 308.

74 Ibid, 207.

75 Charles Zerner quoted in Michael Goldman (ed), *Privatizing Nature: Political Struggles for the Global Commons* (Transnational Institute Series, Pluto Press 1998) 145.

76 Reid and others; ten Kate and Laird; Kerry ten Kate and Sarah A Laird, *The Commercial Use of Biodiversity* (Earthscan 1999).

77 Cancun Declaration (n.58).

Chapter 4

The genetic gold rush

But how do we know when irrational exuberance has unduly escalated asset values?[1]

In 1949, the North asserted that the South was underdeveloped, an invention that, once accepted, spawned a series of strategies, projects, and programmes to overcome this deficiency at great cost and with decidedly adverse results.[2] Forty years later, during the early days of CBD's operation, it was again explained to the South how it was underutilizing its biological and genetic resources, and once more this was accepted, under an equation of development with integration within global markets,[3] and specifically a posited new economy of biodiversity, i.e., a bioeconomy. For the grand bargain to have ever been concluded, this problematization of biodiversity as an under-utilized resource needed to have been accepted.

This chapter recounts the spread of this conviction that biodiversity was under-utilized and, indeed, that there existed a profitable global bioeconomy, leading to a veritable genetic gold[4] rush in the 1990s. It addresses the manifestation of the belief in genetic gold in a series of prescriptive texts, technical and policy manuals, and strategy papers of the 1990s. The chapter examines the early 'biodiversity as biological resources' problematizations of the World Bank, the celebrated INBio-Merck arrangement, the bioprospecting, which is regarded in the literature as ground zero for the rush. The chapter also addresses the impact of these initiatives on the convention, i.e., on the use of biodiversity in international law. All these instances can be viewed as manifestations of the idea of genetic gold, but they also offer slightly different problematizations of biodiversity and different aims in terms of making productive use of biodiversity.

While the allure of genetic gold was never as charismatic, convincing, and all-encompassing as Truman's well-recited declaration of 'underdevelopment' in 1949, there is a certain commonality in the themes that resurface and resonate: losing out due to not tapping into the full economic potential of resources, as reflected in the rhetoric of the LMMC group highlighted in the previous chapter, a call to embrace different and more modern modes of thinking and

62 The genetic gold rush

living, the promise of a better future together in an international community (pointedly without the need for equivalent global commons).

The perception of the convention as a grand bargain laid the groundwork for the genetic gold rush. The former was a representation of international environmental law as a governmental programme in response to a problematization of development. The genetic gold rush represented a wider uptake of the same problematization across the Global South.

During the negotiation and subsequent operation of the biodiversity convention, multiple ideas of biodiversity and responses to its problematizations were advanced. When it came to the integration of conservation and resource management concerns with the very governance of the Global South, biodiversity became entangled within the construction of actual paths to sustainable development.

World Bank's biodiversity: biological resources

The possibility of biodiversity's unrealized economic value as a set of resources brought the attention of economic institutions. A series of seemingly valuable reserves, concentrated in the Global South, required management. The World Bank, which was one of the first global institutions to enthusiastically embrace sustainable development,[5] rose to the challenge of providing guidance regarding the management of biodiversity as a resource.

The first major outcome of its engagement in the biodiversity field was a collaboration between the World Bank and Northern environmental NGOs, which produced a jointly prepared report entitled *Conserving the World's Biological Diversity*.[6] It was commented that 'if Wilson's book is the founding document of the biodiversity discourse, this is the basic policy paper of the global resource managers',[7] and critiqued as 'this document is traditional World Bank policy trimmed up with some remarks on the value of traditional knowledge'.[8]

The report defines biological diversity as 'the total of genes, species and ecosystems on Earth', and biological *resources* 'as the portion of diversity of actual or potential use to people'.[9] These resources – the 'raw materials' for different human communities and the 'planet's life support system' – are being rapidly eroded because of the 'combined destructive impacts of a poor majority struggling to stay alive and an affluent resource-consuming minority'.[10] This dichotomy in the ever-increasing human population is underpinned by a particular geography of biodiversity, whereby 'the tropics harbour a major proportion of the planet's biological diversity' upon which 'the industrialized countries' also rely as 'raw material' for a variety of uses. So far, however, 'the exploitation of the tropics by the industrialized societies has yielded great benefits without making commensurate investments in conservation and without paying the environmental costs of over-exploitation'.[11] This is reflected in 'cheap labour, raw materials with low prices that do not reflect their true value, inappropriate development aid, and the control of commodity prices and interest rates, among other factors'[12] leading to significant resource depletion and environmental destruction.

The report's starting position thus appears to concur with the CBD's notion of a grand bargain, in the sense that 'the problems of conserving biological diversity...cannot be separated from the larger issues of social and economic development'.[13] So biodiversity is firmly placed within an international context, as per the title of the report itself. For conservation endeavours to succeed and these biological resources to be managed so as to 'make their best contribution to sustainable development',[14] biodiversity would have 'to compete for the attention of government and commercial decision-makers'[15] and 'to demonstrate *in economic terms* the contribution biological resources make to the country's social and economic development'.[16]

According to the report, this clearly means attempting at least some valuation, in monetary terms, of biological resources. This valuation will include the use values of natural product, whether consumed directly or commercially exploited, as well as 'ecosystem functions', e.g., soil and water filtration. The report even extends to include options, i.e., future, value, and existence value of certain species.

The report's problematization of 'conserving the world's biodiversity' is defined by its attempt to locate and promote 'cooperative efforts to address the social and economic foundations of resource depletion'.[17] Cooperative here means including the public and private sector, as well as adjustments to local conditions. There are multiple 'partners' – nominally on equal standing – in this new cooperative project: the national governments, development and environmental agencies, the non-governmental sector, but also the 'marketplace',[18] as well as local and indigenous communities.

The solutions contained therein are what have become the standard in terms of biodiversity conservation: *in situ* protected areas, *ex situ* collections in seed banks, zoos, botanical gardens, and the like, reduction in overall pollution, participation and involvement of local communities in the exploitation of biodiversity, since 'people form the foundation for the sustainable use of biological resources';[19] and, of course, international cooperation in the shape of the CBD, whose negotiation is acknowledged in the report as gaining broad support, including that of the US Congress.[20] As recounted in the previous chapter, such support swiftly evaporated once the full scale of the technology transfer provisions came to light.

As recognized from the early days of 'biological diversity', the report runs into the same aspect of the problem, which is the setting of priorities in conservation, given financial, political, economic, capacity, and other constraints. The question of priorities remaining open at this stage can be interpreted as a failure of sorts of the original problematizations of biodiversity, which provided an overall aim, but no way to sort through practical priorities down the chain. According to the report, 'no generally accepted scheme' for assigning priorities exists, and, crucially, such a scheme is 'neither possible nor advisable'.[21] Instead, certain relativity is to be introduced: 'different organizations and institutions can be expected to have different ways of establishing priorities because of their differing goals'.[22] The theme of composing a whole system from disparate parts is reinforced by this conception.

It is further interesting to note the difference, in the narrative of the executive summary, between the section on the threats to biodiversity and the section on the approaches to conserving it. The difference serves to emphasize how the report's 'cooperative approach' was seen as a more constructive response to the problem of biodiversity loss. On the one hand, existing environmental law and conservation practices are problematized within the context of the general identification of threats: 'enacting laws, closing access to resources and declaring additional protected areas' are characterized as 'defensive and often confrontational actions', 'seldom really sufficient to change the social and economic causes of the threats to biological diversity'.[23] On the other hand, in the next section on solutions and approaches, there is only ever discussion of national and government *policies* for conservation, protection, and the like. It is difficult not to infer from this clear categorization of law and policy certain positive and enabling aspects attached to the latter, but not the former.

This trajectory away from state-centric and law-centric solutions, and towards market-oriented solutions, is further supported by the treatment of the financial aspects of biodiversity conservation by the report. It argues that biodiversity conservation 'should be supported to the maximum extent possible through the marketplace...that needs to be established through appropriate policies of the central government'.[24] Such market-based approaches at the domestic level include levies for ecosystem services, 'returning profits from exploitation of biological resources',[25] and environmental conditionalities, among others. At the international level, approaches include funding provided by conventions such as the CBD and other organizations and debt for nature swaps, among others.

The report included a call to construct an additional form of combined biological, economic, and managerial knowledge and practice to support the new goal of managing biodiversity as a resource, as well as the innovative funding mechanisms proposed in the report. It called existing knowledge 'woefully inadequate' and regarded 'developing and using information is therefore an essential part of conservation at all levels, from the local to the global community'.[26]

The World Bank presented a policy manual proposing 'novel approaches, new financial mechanisms, and new policies', as well as the inclusion of new partners.[27] Conserving biodiversity was firmly associated with the management of biological resources. In a way, the report redefined the definition itself of biodiversity conservation, now associated with resource management, i.e., what became sustainable utilization in the language of the CBD. Biodiversity discourse had certainly discovered the world and was elevated to the international plane; now the political question of the relation between biodiversity and development was being addressed directly. Biodiversity was being problematized as a broader object of government: biodiversity reason put in the service of achieving the goal of sustainable development.

Prospectors in 'Canaan': the INBio experiment and the discovery of genetic gold

Costa Rica's favourable geographical location and unique topography enabled the construction of an image of Costa Rica as an ecological tropical paradise, perpetuated by conservation biologists for decades;[28] a *Canaan* for biodiversity 'representing nearly 5 per cent of all the world's diversity of organisms'.[29] This made the state an ideal location for an experiment and 'pilot project' in new approaches to biodiversity conservation.[30]

This geography juxtaposed with the state's development needs created the challenge of designing the correct pursuit of sustainable development, taken to mean, in this context, the pursuit of development without reliance on the continued erosion of this natural 'patrimony'. Costa Rica had established protected areas, with nearly a third of its territory having such conservation status. However, biodiversity needed to make a more dynamic contribution to economic development. Bioprospecting was considered one of the principal ways for making such a contribution. In fact, Costa Rica became the site for a landmark experiment in such practice.

In 1990, Costa Rica established the National Biodiversity Institute (INBio)[31] as an organization separate from the ministry engaging in bioprospecting-related activities, namely 'biodiversity inventorying and monitoring, bioinformatics, education and bioliteracy, wildland management and bioprospecting'.[32] Based on the terms of its operation and its collaborative agreement with the Ministry of Environment and Energy, these activities generally only took place in Costa Rica's designated protected areas, 'which have no inhabitants, local farmers or indigenous people'.[33]

INBio was driven by Daniel Janzen, who was personally involved in its inception and remained influential in its operation:

> His stamp is ineradicable. His language and ideas infiltrate the recesses of INBio. He designs and teaches the parataxonomists courses. He confesses to being INBio's chief cheerleader and fundraiser – its link to the outside world, upon which INBio depends in its inchoate form for its operating budget...He has also kept himself somewhat under wraps in Costa Rica...most Costa Ricans, including newspaper reporters covering INBio, have never heard of Dan Janzen.[34]

Other 'luminaries' of biodiversity, such as Edward Wilson and Thomas Lovejoy, have been members of the institute's international advisory board. Such links position the institute as a major early application of biodiversity

66 The genetic gold rush

reason on the ground, in an area with significant conservation needs, as well as genetic and economic potential.

During the same period, Thomas Eisner's pioneering work in establishing the scientific field of chemical ecology was branching out into conservation, with a proposal to turn the practice of searching or 'prospecting' for bioactive chemicals as a funding mechanism for conservation.[35] Eisner's proposal was to institute a positive, incentivizing, *feedback loop*, whereby the economic returns from the discovery and commercialization of such chemicals would be reinvested back into conservation. This would, in turn, incentivize more conservation of biodiversity as a resource base for the discovery of new chemicals. This notion of a feedback loop would form the conceptual basis of what became known as bioprospecting.[36] Eisner's assumed feedback loop hinged upon the rapid expansion and eventual ubiquitous use of bioprospecting contracts or similar access arrangements to structure this new bioeconomy, capture economic value, and return some of the benefits to the South.

Pilot schemes for the transfer of benefits directly to those local communities close to biodiversity reserves in the South were already being enacted by the mid-1980s by botanical institutions in the UK[37] and various research institutions in the US.[38] But Eisner's contribution, and, in particular, Costa Rica's INBio would prove pivotal.[39] At a conference organized by Eisner at Cornell University in October 1990, Rodrigo Gamez, the representative of INBio, Daniel Janzen, and a representative of the Merck pharmaceutical corporation were brought together.[40]

As a result of this meeting, INBio secured the first bioprospecting contract with a private partner,[41] signed with Merck one year later. The agreement provided the pharmaceutical corporation with access to Costa Rica's biological and genetic resources (specifically samples from plants, insects, and microorganisms collected by the institute from Costa Rica's protected forests) and the right to use those samples in the development of new patented pharmaceutical products, in exchange for an initial lump sum of approximately US$1 million (to cover start-up costs for the sample collection), as well as for future royalties from any commercial products from samples collected under this two-year programme.[42] It was envisaged that this set up was to provide funding and technology for the long term cataloguing of Costa Rica's biodiversity, the operational costs of the institute, as well as other conservation activities.[43]

Bioprospecting, the search for commercially viable plants, organisms, genes, and chemicals, was conceived almost as an additional form of land use, an alternative to other intensive and destructive uses that eliminated the biodiversity reserves. Tapping biodiversity as a set of genetic resources required realizing its inherently economic value – to be 'generated wherever the generative and transformative productivity of living entities can be instrumentalized along lines which make them useful for human projects'.[44] A significant part of biodiversity could in this way become conceived as 'tradable commodities which are subject to market exchange and the assumptions of neoclassical economics'.[45]

The conception of biodiversity as genetic resources was building upon the World Bank's notion of biological resources, towards a more directly commercial and thus private-oriented approach.[46]

This was undoubtedly a market-oriented approach, according to any legal classification. The approach did partly privatize biodiversity as genetic resources, 'packaged' in sample form as genetic information, and sold on the market. It did not privatize the public land where the biodiversity reserves were located, nor did it replace or obviate environmental laws and regulations related to their management. This balance between public–private element was very much a product of its time, a tangible example of the shift from command-and-control environmental legislation to the more flexible era of regulation.[47] The specific legal innovation was the proposition that a commercial contract could constitute an effective and sufficient tool for achieving environmental goals.

Gamez, as the head of INBio, was even more ambitious. In a 'quest for a human sustainable development model',[48] he elevated bioprospecting to the level of 'another type of...very sophisticated agriculture',[49] with genetic samples as its own *sui generis* crop, that would possibly compete and outperform existing intensive uses such as agriculture, economically and environmentally. The economic potential of biodiversity as a set of genetic resources transformed Costa Rica's ecological paradise into reservoirs of untapped resources. With such a possibility in mind, biodiversity conservation became associated with the production of a valuable – and commercially viable – crop, this 'genetic gold' capable of competing effectively with other agricultural or forestry product.

Bioprospecting-as-agriculture would provide the raw material for a host of new medicines, crops, and other chemicals benefiting the whole world, delivering substantial profit for Northern companies and sustainable development for the Global South.[50] No other mode of environmental intervention could compare with such win-win scenarios and offer comparable social and economic benefits in the pursuit of sustainable development. With such promise, it is little wonder that bioprospecting was for a time touted as a newly established biodiversity paradigm and development model. In other words, genetic gold was the symbol of a programme of technological and commercial practices related to a conceived light use of biodiversity as genetic resources in response to a problematization of biodiversity that regarded conservation as insufficient.

Although no commercial products, and hence royalties, ever materialized from this arrangement, Merck's willingness to pay for access and the basic agreement structure of a range of different benefits would significantly influence treaty negotiations, as well as the biodiversity convention's access and benefit sharing provisions. The arrangement with Merck 'was widely hailed as the example of what the Convention would do'[51] and as a 'watershed' in the history of bioprospecting.[52]

68 The genetic gold rush

By consequence, the prospect of similar agreements to 'produce' and sell biodiversity as genetic resources was highly touted. They were elevated – for a time – to the status of major instruments for allocating investment in environment and development, with benefits envisaged across the local, national, and global levels. They would be able to:

Contribute greatly to environmentally sound development and return benefits to the custodians of genetic resources – the national public at large, the staff of conservation units, the farmers, the forest dwellers, and the indigenous people who maintain or tolerate the resources involved.[53]

According to this rationality, biodiversity would constitute both a physical and an intellectual asset; that it represents different forms of capital (or a natural capital to be thought of and used in different ways) to be managed and invested. The mantra of INBio became the oft-used catchphrase '*save it, know it, use it*' – alternatively 'study it, value it, utilize it', which, in turn, became the slogan of Costa Rica's *National Biodiversity Conservation and Sustainable Use Strategy* in 2000.[54] A whole bioprospecting programme could thus be envisaged on the basis of the problematization of biodiversity as precisely such an under-utilized resource.

The holistic character of this programme represented its unique selling point. In addition to the commercial project of extracting economic value from biodiversity reserves, it was further envisaged that the institute would be part of a broader programme of 'biocultural restoration',[55] whereby nature, assuming the label of biodiversity, is used to address social problems. In its early formulations, this restorative axis was plagued by the patronizing portrayals of the Global South reminiscent of conservation biology's earlier efforts to incorporate social concerns the conservation problematization: For 'tropical people... experiencing...intellectual deprivation represented by the upcoming obliteration of tropical wildlands',[56] 'biodiversity must again be a grand intellectual resource...who otherwise lack intellectual challenges and cultural opportunities.'[57]

The enthusiasm surrounding the genetic gold programme, as manifested in the INBio experiment, was palpable. Here was a novel environmental programme, designed and run in a Southern country, through which a Southern state was forging its own sustainable development path, but also in line with World Bank policies and the CBD; taking active control of its natural resources, participating in global markets, and improving both its welfare and environment; a true win–win scenario. There was real commitment to this goal, and what this goal represented in terms of making productive use of biodiversity for the Global South.

The INBio-Merck partnership was also agreed while the negotiations for the CBD were ongoing. The contrast between the positive, win–win attitude of the Merck-INBio collaboration and the negative contestation occurring during international negotiations also did not go unnoticed: 'the cooperative spirit that encompasses...the transaction stands in stark contrast to the divisiveness between North and South which has characterized the negotiations on the Convention.'[58] The biotechnology industry endorsed the initiative and even went as far as to question whether a multilateral treaty was even needed, given the prototype solution presented by the private bioprospecting contract and the INBio experiment.[59] The latter was seen as presenting a pragmatic, practical, business oriented, and industry-friendly approach – everything that the 'old' centres of environmental law and policy up to that point in time (academia, international treaty system, the large environmental Northern NGOs) did not. Theirs was a different problematization.

Starting with straightforward environmental concerns, INBio moved on to the relation between people and resources and ultimately the very political economy of its host country. This was undoubtedly an ambitious undertaking, incorporating elements such as the privatization of certain genetic resources, enabling their sale in global markets, and recognizing the contract concluded between two private parties as a legitimate instrument of environmental law and policy. This was quite different from the discussion of universal resources and the principle of common heritage. The institute was attempting to forge a new relation between biodiversity and Costa Rican society, through the creation of a new bioeconomy tailored for Costa Rican society. This institute's ambitious agenda could be interpreted as seeking nothing sort of an alternative development model, to the point of seeking to replicate with genetic gold what other states had accomplished with oil extraction.[60] The INBio experiment sought to governmentalize biodiversity in a Southern context, by transforming it into an economic resource, into genetic gold, that could not only pay its own way in terms of conservation, but could serve as the foundation for a different society. In this context, biodiversity was conceived as a problem of government from the perspective of (sustainable) development.

Despite the great promises of the genetic gold programme, a question that lingered throughout its heyday was related precisely to the original problematization of biodiversity loss. This was because the direct conservation benefits of these bioprospecting arrangements were dubious and their environmental priorities unclear. They were a type of business transaction based on a particular supply and demand of a niche resource; no private enterprise or research institution would conclude a bioprospecting agreement with a locale that did not contain significant reserves of undocumented biodiversity, irrespective of how environmentally endangered an ecosystem, habitat, or species within it was. The focus would be on sufficient sample collection, in order to discover undocumented and potentially useful or valuable organisms and genes.

This was not the previous environmentalism revolving around the image of the activist, ecologically minded scientist trying their hand at pressuring for stricter environmental laws, or the top-down bargaining between Northern and Southern blocs at international fora. The institute, as a good fundraiser

70 The genetic gold rush

and entrepreneur, had gone out and located a willing business partner, in the shape of a large multinational corporation, willing to actually pay for access to a resource that was previously considered 'undeveloped'. Even though the specific INBio–Merck contract did not yield that special and profitable commercial product, the overall perception of success created expectations that others would follow, thus solidifying the creation of a new global market for genetic resources and bioeconomy. Through the discovery of genetic gold, the pursuit of sustainable development through the use of biodiversity could be observed in action.

Manuals for a new bioeconomy

Under conditions of enthusiasm for the INBio experiment, the wider potential of bioprospecting, and the genetic gold programme as a whole, the first decade of the CBD was accompanied by, and in a certain sense had to compete with, high-profile applied policy manuals with instructions on taking advantage, managing, and realising the full economic potential of biodiversity as a set of resources, biological and genetic.[61] A significant composite policy intervention was the *Global Biodiversity Strategy*, assembled by the World Resources Institute (WRI), IUCN, and UNEP from 1989 to 1992, in consultation with FAO and UNESCO.[62] The lineage of genetic gold, and, in particular, the INBio experiment outlined in the preceding section, is evident in its subtitle: *Guidelines for Action to Save, Study, and Use Earth's Biotic Wealth Sustainably and Equitably*. The World Bank supported the development of this strategy, which it understood as 'a strategy that defines the basic problems and agrees to appropriate objectives'.[63]

Among these works, a seminal contribution in terms of genetic gold was *Biodiversity Prospecting: Using Genetic Resources for Sustainable Development*,[64] the contribution of WRI to the *Global Biodiversity Strategy* that drew directly from the Costa Rican experience and the INBio–Merck experiment. This report proposed designs for the 'new kinds of organizations, contracts and laws needed to ensure that both human communities and their natural surroundings benefit from the bioprospecting boom'.[65]

The core of this manual's rationality is encapsulated in the clever heading of the first chapter, *A New Lease on Life*. A subtle play on words, the triple meaning of 'life' in the phrase – i.e., as genetic resources, the environment in general, as well as the welfare of Southern society – implies that a new lease *on* life (i.e., according to the manual, market-oriented reforms for attracting investment opportunities in bioprospecting) would be a new lease *of* life for both nature and society in the South. This promising rhetoric of the future was grounded in the 'flurry of interest and enthusiasm in biodiversity prospecting',[66] at least partly due to the perceived success of the INBio experiment. An overwhelming sense of a historic shift occurring was prevalent in the instructions; a promise that the 'true economic potential'[67] of biodiversity was on the verge of being realized.

The manual provided the first comprehensive set of guidelines specifically for managing biodiversity *as* genetic gold. To turn this promise of genetic gold into reality, an identified national 'policy vacuum'[68] across the countries that hold valuable genetic resources in terms of the regulation of bioprospecting had to be filled. 'Appropriate policies and institutions are needed to ensure that the commercial value obtained from genetic and biochemical resources is a positive force for development and conservation.'[69] The manual includes a number of proposals to fill this vacuum, focusing on three main areas: setting up INBio-style institutions, shaping bioprospecting contract terms and reforming contract law, and creating appropriate intellectual property rights regimes. These proposals, in some shape or form, found their way onto the CBD and are explored in the next chapter as part of the CBD's own attempts to regulate the new bioeconomy of genetic gold.

This is not a document in the thrall of the exuberance surrounding the genetic gold rush. It acknowledges and warns that 'historically, the exploitation of a "new" resource has led to its exhaustion and to the destruction of local communities and cultures'.[70] In almost the same breath however, it argues in detail, with supporting evidence, that 'there is a growing demand for new genes and chemicals and a growing awareness that an abundant and virtually untapped supply of these resources exits in wildland biodiversity'.[71] The juxtaposition clearly enshrines the impression that the governmental task related to biodiversity is to create the right regulatory environment for taking advantage of the economic and developmental opportunity that biodiversity as a resource represents.

The promise of genetic gold: a new state and a new society

The promise of genetic gold was that it would generally be a worthwhile investment opportunity for the North and an important development opportunity for the South. This was based on the prediction that bioprospecting would consistently yield profitable commercial products, in the form of highly prized pharmaceuticals, modified crops, or other chemicals.

In this particular attempt to cut to the long-standing Gordian knot of the contrast between positive economic development and negative nature conservation, through the cumulative advocacy of biodiversity experts and international organizations and the development appetite of states, biodiversity became intrinsically associated with the opportunity represented by 'genetic gold'. The shifts in problematizations are quite clear: from biodiversity to development, but most importantly from concern about the lack of protection of biodiversity to concern over not making 'proper' use of it. Biodiversity could almost be seen as a resource similar to oil, on which a 'new economy' could be constructed, as alluded to in the Cancun Declaration. There were even whispers of creating a 'biodiversity cartel'[72]

72 The genetic gold rush

of price controls and trade quotas and the formation of new 'eco-states' or 'gene states' (in effect 'reformed' developmental states) in the South, under the guidance of the World Bank.[73]

This was, of course, an ambitious, expansive, and operating at the macro-level, biodiversity programme emerging from the biodiversity problematization. It required the perspective that there is enough economic and political potential in biodiversity as genetic resource to build an alternative development model, by moving away from extractive/raw material provision industries, such as agriculture and logging. Such a view calls for a complete repositioning of biodiversity within global, but not necessarily environmental, politics. It seems to imply that in addition to oil states, there can almost be a different type of post-colonial state, organized around the sustainable utilization of biodiversity. The not so subtle celebration of Costa Rica in the literature resolutely pointed to such an implicit image.

This model was centralized to the extent that its envisions itself as an environmentally benign, sustainable alternative to the developmental state; a state-led and pre-defined set of developmental policies, with minor forms of devolution to localities, private entities, and civil society. However, such a project inevitably applies only to certain states within the recognized biodiversity hotspots of the world, but even in those instances the proposal that the market-oriented management of natural reserves would become another form of agriculture rivalling existing agricultural practices has not been proven correct. Finally, biodiversity as genetic gold has not been a natural resource to rival oil, gas, or water. In this ambitious and top-down format, then, this political project of genetic gold has failed.

There is, however, another understanding of the function of genetic gold that is less ambitious in terms of macro-level, state-based, political rhetoric, but derived from existing practices, bottom-up and diffuse. Genetic gold here refers to a different method of allocating investment in natural and human capital. In this guise, the empowerment of individuals and communities is seen as a more efficient and effective intervention or policy, based on the increasing cost of enforcing environmental law (especially the top-down international variety), not only measured in economic terms but also in terms of declining political and social authority and legitimacy.[74]

In this frame, the genetic gold programme prescribes a liberalization and deregulation of environmental intervention. We are in the terrain of Article 11 of the CBD, whereby states are asked to provide incentives for the conservation and sustainable use of biodiversity. This is considered a realist or pragmatic attempt to enable the market to provide additional sources of funding and additional incentives to invest in biodiversity. The new bioeconomy structured around genetic gold appears as a variation of sustainable development that places importance on individuals and local communities that, via INBio-style institutions, will venture on the market in search of the next access and benefit sharing (ABS) contract.

From funding to finance

The symbol of the promise of genetic gold is the transition from the problematization of conservation to the problematization of findings pathways to achieve sustainable development. The World Bank heralded this shift in the 1992 report discussed in the first section of this chapter, when it urged states to 'recognize the many values of biological resources, and *take advantage of opportunities to invest in the continued productivity* that such resources require', as well as creating the appropriate tax and investment climate for non-state actors to invest in such opportunities to manage biological resources.[75] Similar problematizations were also being formulated elsewhere; the chapter explores the influential INBio experiment, whose initial success influenced the *Global Biodiversity Strategy*, the CBD itself, and a proliferation of policy manuals seeking to take advantage of the opportunity represented by biodiversity as genetic gold.

Even if the negativity associated with conservation was somehow overcome, the elephant in the room of any biodiversity convention and/or related global regime has always been the economic cost and hence the required additional funding for the expansive conservation activities it intimates.[76] The designation and management of protected areas is an expensive undertaking, and often seen as doubly so, in the sense of both funding the active management required and foregoing income from further land development. Developed countries agreed to provide 'new and additional financial resources' to meet the 'full incremental costs' of implementation of the treaty's objectives.[77] A financial mechanism was set up to administer these additional funds,[78] run by the Global Environment Facility under the guidance of the conference of the parties.[79] In the treaty text, implementation by developing countries was then made explicitly dependent on the provision of these funds, as well as the more controversial technology transfer commitments discussed in the previous chapter.[80] These provisions reinforce the notion that there was an unstated treaty aim of achieving some equitable balancing between North and South in this area, and also strengthen the perception of the treaty as a 'grand bargain'.

Based on such and other similar arrangements from conservation treaties, the international community currently spends $4 to $10 billion per year on biodiversity conservation.[81] This is not and has never been considered sufficient for the ambitious targets set by the CBD's strategic plans. Consequently, a funding gap has accompanied the biodiversity regime since its inception. The regime constitutes a perpetual search for biodiversity funding. It was first envisaged that some of the shortfall would be picked up indirectly, through the promise of genetic gold. The elusive search for private biodiversity financing continues to the present day. It is presently believed that this shortfall would be picked up by the recognition of the economic value of ecosystem services.

Genetic gold, however, raised the specific and foundational question of how biodiversity conservation should be funded in the first place. The

74 The genetic gold rush

problematization *de facto* advocated moving away from the traditional state-centric initial financial arrangements of the biodiversity convention, and towards the search for private funding, i.e., *financing*.[82] The problem here related to which activity is preferable, and by extension how it should be financed. The implication being that lack of finance/investment means that this activity is not desirable, and thus the market (as opposed to the international community) is used to make resource allocation and distribution decisions. The promise of genetic gold transcends the search for bridging funding gaps for conservation activities, both domestically and internationally. It promises that always limited conservation funding can be transformed into a much wider prospect of biodiversity finance.

By extension, the posing of this question is linked to overcoming anti-market or anti-economic sentiments. The negativity attached to markets and biodiversity ownership by the problematization of the irresponsible state requiring decisive international intervention is in this problematization completely reversed, whereby resource ownership and management is welcomed; private solutions are welcomed against public ones.

Striking at the heart of the environment versus development binary, the call of genetic gold emerged as a sustainable development-infused problematization that became inveigled with the concurrent attempts to negotiate the CBD and then begin its operation in the early to mid-1990s. This chapter illustrated that the whole endeavour was not simply a fight over the control of another set of valuable natural resources, but a debate over the relation between two objects of governing (biodiversity and the Global South) and their combined problematization.

When Edward Wilson was declaring that 'biological diversity must be treated more seriously as a global resource, to be indexed, used and above all, preserved',[83] he did not envision that, once this call was answered, biodiversity would indeed be a global resource to be, above all, exploited, rather than preserved, for the benefit of humanity first.

Notes

1 Alan Greenspan, 'The Challenge of Central Banking in a Democratic Society'. Francis Boyer Lecture of The American Enterprise Institute for Public Policy Research, Washington, D.C. December 5, 1996. Available at: https://www.federalreserve.gov /boarddocs/speeches/1996/19961205.htm.

2 Gustavo Esteva, 'Development' in Wolfgang Sachs (ed), *The Development Dictionary: A Guide to Knowledge as Power* (2nd edn, Zed Books 2010).

3 Gertrand Berthoud, 'Market' in Wolfgang Sachs (ed), *The Development Dictionary: A Guide to Knowledge as Power* (Zed books 1991).

4 Kathleen McAfee, 'Selling Nature to Save it? Biodiversity and Green Developmentalism' (1999) 17 *Environment and Planning D: Society and Space* 133, 146–8.

5 Alexander Gillespie, *The Illusion of Progress: Unsustainable Development in International Law and Policy* (Earthscan 2001) 12.

The genetic gold rush 75

6 Jeffrey A. McNeely and others, *Conserving the World's Biological Diversity* (IUCN 1990).
7 Michael Flitner, 'Biodiversity: Of Local Commons and Global Commodities' in Michael Goldman (ed), *Privatizing Nature: Political Struggles for the Global Commons* (Pluto Press 1998) 148.
8 Ibid.
9 McNeely and others (n.6), 11.
10 Ibid.
11 Ibid.
12 Ibid.
13 Ibid.
14 Ibid.
15 Ibid.
16 Emphasis added. Ibid.
17 Ibid, 12.
18 Ibid, 15.
19 Ibid, 13.
20 Ibid, 13.
21 Ibid, 14.
22 Ibid.
23 Ibid, 12.
24 Ibid, 15.
25 Ibid.
26 Ibid, 13.
27 Ibid.
28 Roger Lewin, 'Costa Rican Biodiversity' (1988) 242 *Science* 1637; Laura Tangley, 'Cataloging Costa Rica's Diversity' (1990) 40 *BioScience* 633.
29 Rodrigo Gamez and others, 'Costa Rica's Conservation Program and National Biodiversity Institute (INBio)' in Walter V. Reid and others (eds), *Biodiversity Prospecting: Using Genetic Resources for Sustainable Development* (World Resources Institute (WRI) 1993) (n.29), 77.
30 David Takacs, *The Idea of Biodiversity: Philosophies of Paradise* (The Johns Hopkins University Press 1996), 289.
31 Gamez and others; Daniel H. Janzen, 'How to Save Tropical Biodiversity: The National Biodiversity Institute of Costa Rica' (1991) 37 *American Entomologist* 159.
32 Rodrigo Gamez, 'The Link Between Biodiversity and Sustainable Development: Lessons From INBio's Bioprospecting Programme in Costa Rica' in Charles R. McManis (ed), *Biodiversity and the Law: Intellectual Property, Biotechnology & Traditional Knowledge* (Earthscan 2007), 83.
33 Ibid.
34 Takacs (n.30), 291.
35 Thomas Eisner and Elizabeth A Beiring, 'Biotic Exploration Fund: Protecting Biodiversity through Chemical Prospecting' (1994) 44 *Bioscience* 95; Thomas Eisner, 'Chemical Prospecting: A Global Imperative' (1994) 138; *Proceedings of the American Philosophical Society* 385; Thomas Eisner, 'Chemical Prospecting: A Proposal for Action' in F.H. Bormann and S.R. Kellert (eds), *Ecology, Economics, Ethics: The Broken Circle* (Yale University Press 1991); Thomas Eisner, 'Prospecting for Nature's Chemical Riches' (1990) 6 *Issues in Science and Technology* 31.
36 Asebey, Edgar J. and Kempenaar, Jill D., ''Biodiversity Prospecting: Fulfilling the Mandate of the Biodiversity Convention' (1995) 28 *Vanderbilt Journal of International Law* 703; Reid, Walter V., et al., *Biodiversity Prospecting: Using Genetic Resources for Sustainable Development* (World Resources Institute, USA, 1993).

76 The genetic gold rush

37 E.g., National History Museum, Kew Gardens, and the London Zoo. See Fiona McConnell, *The Biodiversity Convention: A Negotiating History* (Kluwer Law International 1996), 39.

38 The earlier National Cancer Institute programme for drug discovery began in 1986, while the International Cooperative Biodiversity Groups programme, sponsored by the National Institutes of Health, National Science Foundation, began in 1993. For more information see James S. Miller, 'Impact of the Convention on Biological Diversity: The Lessons from Ten Years of Experience with Models of Equitable Sharing of Benefits' in Charles R. McManis (ed), *Biodiversity and the Law: Intellectual Property, Biotechnology and Traditional Knowledge* (Earthscan 2007).

39 Michele Zebich-Knos, 'Preserving Biodiversity in Costa Rica: The Case of the Merck-INBio Agreement' (1997) 6 *The Journal of Environment & Development* 180.

40 Eisner, 'Chemical Prospecting: A Global Imperative' (n.35), 387.

41 For more information see Miller (n.38).

42 Gamez and others (n.29).

43 10% of the initial start-up fee and 50% of all royalties would go into conservation and protection. See Eisner and Beiring (n.19), 97.

44 Stefan Helmreich, 'Blue-green Capital, Biotechnological Circulation and an Oceanic Imaginary: A Critique of Biopolitical Economy' (2007) *Biosocieties* 287, 295 ff.

45 Kathleen McAfee, 'Neoliberalism on the Molecular Scale: Economic and Genetic Reductionism in Biotechnology Battles' (2003) 34 *Geoforum* 203.

46 Kerry ten Kate and Sarah A Laird, *The Commercial Use of Biodiversity* (Earthscan 1999).

47 On these legal transitions see generally Neil Gunningham, 'Environmental Law, Regulation, and Governance: Shifting Architectures' (2009) 21 *JEL* 179.

48 Gamez (n.32), 77.

49 Quoted in Takacs (n.30), 292.

50 Timothy Swanson, 'The Reliance of Northern Economies on Southern Biodiversity: Biodiversity as Information' (1996) 17 *Ecological Economics* 1, Kerry ten Kate and Sarah A Laird, 'Biodiversity and Business: Coming to Terms with the "Grand Bargain"' (2000) 76 *International Affairs* 241.

51 Michael D. Jr Coughlin, 'Using the Merck-INBio Agreement to Clarify the Convention on Biological Diversity' (1993) 31 *Colum J Transnat'l L* 337, 356.

52 See Walter V. Reid and others, *Biodiversity Prospecting: Using Genetic Resources for Sustainable Development* (World Resources Institute, USA 1993), 1.

53 Ibid, 2.

54 Gamez (n.32), 79.

55 Daniel H. Janzen, 'Tropical Ecological and Biocultural Restoration' (1988) 239 *Science* 243.

56 Ibid, 244.

57 Takacs (n.30), 296.

58 Coughlin (n.51), 357.

59 Or at least by the US biotechnology industry, as stated in ibid, 341.

60 Michael Watts, 'Development and Governmentality' (2003) 24 *Singapore Journal of Tropical Geography* 6.

61 An indicative list includes ten Kate and Laird, *The Commercial Use of Biodiversity*; Sarah A Laird (ed), *Biodiversity and Traditional Knowledge: Equitable Partnerships in Practice* (People and Plants Conservation Series, Earthscan 2002); Reid and others.

62 WRI/IUCN/UNEP, *Global Biodiversity Strategy* (1992).

63 McNeely and others (n.6), 14.

64 Reid and others (n.61).

65 Foreword in ibid.

66 Ibid, 2.

67 Ibid, 1.
68 Ibid, 2.
69 Ibid, 3.
70 Ibid, 6.
71 Ibid, 6 *ff.*
72 Tilford, David S., 'Saving the Blueprints: The International Legal Regime for Plant Resources' (1998) 30 *Case Western Reserve Journal of International Law* 373, 436–40
73 Michael Goldman, 'Eco-governmentality and Other Transnational Practices of a "Green" World Bank' in Richard Peet and Michael Watts (eds), *Liberation Ecologies: Environment, Development, Social Movements* (2nd edn, Routledge 2004).
74 This understanding of genetic gold is analyzed in Andreas Kotsakis, 'Change and Subjectivity in International Environmental Law: The Micro-Politics of the Transformation of Biodiversity into Genetic Gold' (2014) 3 *TEL* 127.
75 McNeely and others (n.6), 15.
76 This preoccupation is prevalent already in accounts of the early days of negotiation and the convention's operation, such as Simone Bilderbeek (ed), *Biodiversity and International Law: The Effectiveness of International Environmental Law* (IOS Press 1992); McConnell.
77 CBD, Art. 20.
78 CBD, Art. 21
79 The collaboration was established on a formal, legal basis through a memorandum of understanding between the two institutions. See UNEP/CBD/COP/3/Decision III.8 (1996).
80 CBD, Art. 20(4).
81 Edward P. Barbier and others, 'How to Pay for Saving Biodiversity: Can Private Sector Involvement in a Global Agreement Help to Conserve Global Biodiversity?' (2018) 360 *Science* 486 (n.75), 487.
82 Michael C. Rubino, 'Biodiversity Finance' (2000) 76 *International Affairs* 223; Barbier and others.
83 Edward O. Wilson (ed), *BioDiversity* (National Academy Press 1988), 3.

Chapter 5

The regulation of genetic gold

When you want to know how things really work, study them when they're coming apart[1]

The impact of genetic gold on international environmental law and the biodiversity convention can be observed in the rise of the access and benefit sharing acronym, ABS, in the operation of the biodiversity convention, a rise confirmed ten years ago by the adoption of the additional Nagoya Protocol. This was despite the fact that the initial language and conceptual construction of the treaty centred on the primary aim of biodiversity conservation and did not explicitly envisage such a protocol, as was the case with the Cartagena protocol governing the handling and transfer of genetically modified organisms.[2] The ABS acronym was not even used in the first conferences of the parties, as there was no agreement yet on the process for implementing the third objective of benefit sharing or even on the constituent elements of what subsequently became ABS.[3] In the midst of a genetic gold rush, however, the pursuit of that third treaty objective assumed increasing importance.[4] The conference of the parties then affirmed, at an early stage, that 'the CBD is grounded on mutual reliance on fair and equitable sharing for the prosperity of all humankind'.[5] In the end, ABS mechanisms were the direct result of the genetic gold rush, and the treaty's third objective is interpreted through such a prism – of distributing the benefits of genetic gold fairly and equitably.

For the purposes of this genealogical analysis, it does not matter that the genetic gold rush burst like any other economic bubble. It was the belief and commitment to this bioeconomy that produced significant transformation in biodiversity law at all levels, from the international to the local. What matters is the governmental thought that genetic gold produced and its contribution to biodiversity reason, which is distinct from the success or eventual failure of the real political project of genetic gold.

This chapter will explore this response of the CBD to the problematization of biodiversity represented by the idea of genetic gold. At a surface level, this response consisted of a legal instrument that marshalled the ABS acronym into a type of regulatory mechanism for the bioeconomy of genetic gold. The contribution of the CBD's genetic gold programme to the overall biodiversity reason is the confirmation of an underlying grid of rationality, whereby biodiversity is to be used to achieve economic, political, or social ends.

Law and genetic gold

The CBD had provided a legal foundation for the establishment a global bioeconomy, when it confirmed the removal of biodiversity from any commons and the principle of national sovereignty over it as a resource.[6] The treaty also confirmed the concept of genetic resources.[7]

On the basis of this legal ground, within a seven-year span from 1995 to 2002, over 100 states, possessing the majority of the world's remaining biodiversity, introduced various regulations regulating and *de facto* restricting access to genetic resources.[8] The exuberance of the genetic gold rush had a marked legal effect, as predicted by the World Bank's 1992 finding of a 'policy vacuum' in this area; newly self-aware biodiversity-rich states scrambled to protect this newly discovered valuable resource – to protect it not from an environmental, but from an economic and investment perspective. Even if the envisaged biodiversity cartel never materialized, there was still a rapid proliferation of regional, national, and sub-national biodiversity laws, regulations, and policies.

This legal phenomenon then became understood and framed as a problem of market regulation, framed in terms of international trade and foreign investment. These legal practices, separate from the international treaty, became a target of problematization. First and foremost, these regulations were often in explicit and direct contrast to the treaty provisions requiring them to facilitate access[9] and, of course, conserve biodiversity, as the primary objective. The focus was on the need to control access to valuable genetic resources, on the basis of national sovereignty. In other words, they were concerned with establishing a legal basis for the pursuit of the bioeconomy promised by the idea of genetic gold. Second, rapidly proliferating national biodiversity laws had produced an additional heterogeneous tableau of divergent access requirements and sustainable use provisions tailored to regional, national, and local perceptions of the correct path for fostering development through genetic gold. The CBD's 'hold' of biodiversity, and crucially its primary problematization as global biodiversity, was being weakened.

Some related regional initiatives of that period, such as the Andean pact's decision 391[10] and the more broadly themed African Model Law,[11] received attention for their attempt to address the problems of national and *ad hoc* approaches to ABS legislation on genetic resources. These constituted specialized soft law aiming for some modicum of harmonization and legislative convergence on the issue of access to and management of genetic resources, as well as the distribution of benefits from their utilization, but largely ignoring or

80   The regulation of genetic gold

paying token attention to other biodiversity components and CBD aims, such as biodiversity conservation.

The CBD, of course, relied on national implementation, having created only minimal international obligations for its signatories. But the connection between these separate national and regional initiatives and the CBD's objectives was at times tenuous. These types of laws were taking the biodiversity project further away from the conservation imperative. Furthermore, moving past environmental concerns and law, this legislative rush was expected to foster destructive regulatory competition, especially between neighbouring states with similar genetic resources, leading to a 'race to the bottom', a reciprocal lowering of standards in order to attract foreign investment in the resource.[12] Once the problem was framed along such regulatory lines, some form of 'joint regulatory framework'[13] or other legislative response – in the shape of a harmonized regulatory regime – to this legislative phenomenon induced by the genetic gold rush was needed.[14]

A wider problematization, of the convention itself, also lurked in the background. This was not solely an issue of the relation between international and domestic law and the effects of regulation in terms of attracting foreign investment. The challenge of genetic gold went straight to the heart of the fragile 'grand bargain', this notion of North–South exchange that underpinned the CBD as a whole. The sudden prospect of a new bioeconomy, not fully foreseen by the legal text itself, posed questions for both sides, and exposed the limitations of this grand bargain.

The Global North, always wary of the politicization of international environmental law in general – although no state has reacted as melodramatically as the US – was afraid that the biodiversity convention was becoming a Southern-led initiative, a step towards forced biotechnology transfer and other forms of restitution and redistribution.[15] This fear, abated through the grand bargain long enough to secure agreement, came back with force in the 1990s. Was this a way to subvert the emerging WTO regime? In many ways, this problematization was about the 'proper' place of international environmental law within international law and the global political economy. And equally from the Southern perspective, if biodiversity was such an economically valuable resource, why was the treaty insistent on facilitating and opening access to it? It would then seem that the convention was the opposite of what it claimed to be: 'an initiative of the North to globalize the control, management and ownership of biological diversity so as to ensure free access to the biological resources which are needed as raw material for the biotechnology industry'.[16] The unprecedented potential of genetic gold made both blocs, already quite diverse and heterogeneous in their forced inception, once more suspicious of each other and of their own membership.

The CBD did respond to this complex problematization of domestic and international law, first by adopting the Bonn guidelines and subsequently with the Nagoya protocol on ABS, as recounted in Chapter 1. Legal doctrine tells us that the guidelines and protocol serve the implementation of CBD's third primary objective of fair and equitable benefit sharing. This response saw the CBD assuming the role of a *de facto* regulator for this new bioeconomy that it had (to a certain extent inadvertently) spawned. This chapter charts the parameters of the CBD's overall response to genetic gold, the joint creation of the Bonn Guidelines and the Nagoya Protocol.

ABS regulation

In 2002, the Convention adopted the 'Bonn guidelines on Access to Genetic Resources and Fair and Equitable Sharing of the Benefits Arising out of their Utilization'.[17] These guidelines applied to both genetic resources as genetic material[18] and their derivatives,[19] assigning limited property rights over them.[20] This was a first step. The guidelines were drafted as a voluntary, 'soft-law' instrument, formally marking the first concerted multilateral contribution towards achieving the convention's fair and equitable benefit sharing objective. The ostensibly legal task was to elaborate and expand upon primarily Article 15, laying the groundwork for a future introduction of a standardized process for granting access to genetic resources and sharing of benefits arising from their utilization.

A primary goal was to standardize and harmonize the form of bioprospecting contracts, using standardized material transfer and benefit sharing agreements.[21] The use of standardized contracts is deemed to have a number of advantages in the legal marketplace. These contracts directly empower local communities as stakeholders, provided there is sufficient capacity building for them to take advantage of their stake at the negotiating table. They lower negotiation costs and enhance legal certainty and clarity through harmonization. They simplify dispute settlement with the inclusion of resolution clauses. More generally, they establish a base of reciprocity by outlining a choice of fair and equitable returns for the sale of genetic material.

The Bonn guidelines were also designed as a collection of model legislation to assist primarily Southern states in constructing national regulatory capacity, and for this reason included detailed guidelines regarding the design of ABS mechanisms at various levels. The guidelines were thus directly at aiming to harmonize national and regional law and policy, after the legislative explosion of *ad hoc* regimes during the years 1995–2002. A further significant effect of the Bonn guidelines in terms of the operation of the biodiversity regime was the establishment of the ABS acronym in the language and operation of the treaty regime.

Building on the Bonn guidelines, negotiations commenced on a new ABS regime in 2004, 'with the aim of adopting instrument/instruments to effectively implement Article 15 and Article 8(j), and the three objectives of the Convention'.[22] This process would eventually lead to the adoption of the Nagoya Protocol in 2010.

82 The regulation of genetic gold

The following sections analyze the protocol provisions regarding the ABS mechanism. Emphasis is placed on the scope of application, the basic principles of the ABS process, and the acquisition of an international certificate that will enable the cross-border movement of genetic resources. The failure to agree on a centralized global mechanism for certain types of genetic resources, and the disappointing legal effect of the protocol are also discussed.

Legal basis and scope of application

Genetic resources are defined in the CBD as 'genetic material of actual or potential value',[23] whereas genetic material is defined as 'any material of plant, animal, microbial or other origin containing functional units of heredity'.[24] Genetic resources are further distinguished from the broader category of biological resources, which are defined as including 'organisms or parts thereof, populations, or any other biotic component of ecosystems with actual or potential use or value for humanity'.[25]

The Nagoya protocol adds to the CBD stable of legal definitions. Utilization of genetic resources is specifically defined as 'to conduct research and development on the genetic and/or biochemical composition of genetic resources'.[26] This type of utilization gives rise to a legal obligation to share the benefits with the provider of these resources.[27] Biotechnology is explicitly included in this obligation as a specialized sub-category of utilization defined as 'any technological application that uses biological systems, living organisms, or derivatives thereof, to make or modify products or processes for specific use'.[28] The Protocol specifically mentions that biotechnology can make use of a derivate – i.e., 'a naturally-occurring biochemical compound resulting from the genetic expression or metabolism of biological or genetic resources', even if it constitutes genetic material without functional units of heredity, and thus not legally a genetic resource according to the main treaty – and still create such benefit sharing obligations. There are thus three distinct categories of use recognized: utilization (general R&D), application (biotechnology), and commercialization, that all create an equal obligation to be accompanied by an ABS agreement with the provider of the resource or related knowledge.[29]

In another change in scope, the protocol conceives of the involvement of local and indigenous communities as an integral element of the ABS mechanism. This is a significant change from the original treaty text that worded concern over these communities under the conservation objective.[30] Communities are recognized as holders of genetic resources, provided this recognition stems from 'domestic legislation over [their] established rights',[31] and thus entitled to benefit sharing. At the same time, the utilization of traditional knowledge associated with genetic resources, instead of resources themselves, is equally and separately recognized as a category of utilization also creating a full benefit sharing obligation for the user.[32]

The regulation of genetic gold   83

If the rights of these communities to control their resources and knowledge are established in domestic law, then access to them is dependent on their 'approval and involvement',[33] which may be subject to separate 'criteria and/or processes' compared to the standard process of obtaining prior informed consent.[34] The same provisions generally apply to accessing the traditional knowledge of these communities.[35] In addition, however, communities, based on their customary laws and practices, should develop their own community protocols, minimum mutually agreed terms, and model contractual clauses for ABS, specifically in relation to traditional knowledge,[36] while existing 'customary laws, community protocols and procedures' have to be taken into account in the implementation of ABS legislation.[37] It is important to note that this special treatment is attached solely to ABS provisions regarding traditional knowledge, inferring that agreements on genetic resources will have to follow the more standardized process.

Basic principle and the standard ABS process

The basic principle that underpins the ABS process as conceived by the CBD is that access is only granted subject to the prior informed consent of the country of origin or in general of the provider of the genetic resources.[38] The term 'informed' implies that consent must not be a procedural formality, but instead must be based on as complete as possible information on the process of collection and utilization of the genetic resource and on the negotiation of mutually agreed terms. Applying for access to genetic resources is to be governed by 'fair and non-arbitrary rules and procedures',[39] leading to 'a clear and transparent written decision...in a cost-effective manner and within a reasonable period of time'.[40] States and public and private entities can be both providers and users. The 'provider' of genetic resources is 'the Party providing such resources that is the country of origin of such resources or a Party that has acquired the resources in accordance with the Convention'.[41]

According to the protocol, a procedure for securing the prior informed consent for access and agreement on benefit sharing terms is to be instituted at the national level through legislative, administrative, and policy measures.[42] This is relatively straightforward when access relates to public land owned by the state, but a significant number of the remaining areas of high biodiversity are located in close proximity to traditional or indigenous communities.[43] The protocol takes the later reality fully into account; access would require their additional 'approval and involvement',[44] indicating a different, more detailed, direct and participatory process compared to the granting of access by the relevant competent authority at the national level.[45]

Benefit sharing must be fair and equitable and mutually agreed.[46] Benefits can be both monetary and non-monetary;[47] an indicative list of potential benefits is included in an annex.[48] The terms 'fair and equitable' present a continuing

84 The regulation of genetic gold

difficulty in terms of their legal definition. A 1999 report[49] advanced a somewhat procedural definition of the terms, proposing that 'fair' should relate to a process that achieves 'a proper balance of needs, rights, or demands' and 'equitable' should be associated with an outcome that is based on criteria and indicators for equity. The Bonn guidelines recognized that benefits to be shared will 'vary depending on what is regarded as fair and equitable in light of the circumstances'.[50] There is no further clarification in the protocol. It is safe to argue that these terms are contingent, and determined by the authorities assessing access applications, as well as the private parties in the process of negotiating access.

The types of benefits to be shared, as well as the method and the timing of the sharing process, are open to negotiation. The genetic gold rush constructed the image of such benefits being a financial windfall. Instead, the working group that prepared the protocol considered capacity building as the 'essence of ABS'.[51] The early recognition of the importance of capacity-building can be observed from the outset in the fact that the COP decision mandating the constitution of the ABS working group also includes an action plan on capacity building specifically for ABS.[52]

Capacity-building is considered necessary for adequately negotiating ABS arrangements, particularly when it builds up the negotiating and entrepreneurial capacity of individuals, institutions, and communities as an element of their overall managerial capacity.

Issued access permits are to be transmitted to the ABS Clearing House established by the protocol as part of the convention's overall clearing house mechanism.[53] Once this notification occurs, the permit is then recognized as an 'internationally recognized certificate of compliance'.[54] These certificates form the basis for monitoring through a network of multiple 'designated checkpoints'.[55] Users of genetic resources may be required by law to provide such information to designated checkpoints directly.[56] Information to be collected and made available through these checkpoints includes '*inter alia*, any stage of research, development, innovation, pre-commercialization or commercialization'.[57]

It is also worthwhile to note that in contrast to provisions concerning the competent national authorities issuing the access permits, there is no designated adjective characterizing these checkpoints; therefore, aside from the national level, they may also be constituted at sub-national (e.g., for a single indigenous/ethnic group across national borders) or regional levels (e.g., a single point for the European Union).

This certification system supports the flow of genetic resources in the context of the new bioeconomy of genetic gold. It creates transaction/exchange standards for the operation of the market for these resources, by pairing the granting of an access permit by the provider with a requirement on the user to secure a certificate of compliance.[58]

The (missing) global ABS mechanism

There are genetic resources for which the above ABS process cannot be followed. For them, a different ABS mechanism, following the example of FAO's multilateral system for plant genetic resources, was mooted. The protocol's preamble recognizes that:

> An innovative solution is required to address the fair and equitable sharing of benefits...associated with genetic resources that occur in transboundary situations or for which it is not possible to grant or obtain prior informed consent.

As genetic resources or, indeed, traditional knowledge or indigenous communities may not fall neatly inside the lines of national jurisdiction, overlap and jurisdictional competition over the same resource or knowledge can occur.

This preambular statement harks to an institutional solution already existing under the aegis of FAO. Certain plant genetic resources of importance to food and agriculture are currently held by the network of International Agricultural Research Centres (IARCs) around the world, essentially seed banks managed by the Consultative Group on International Agricultural Research (CGIAR),[59] which is, in turn, governed by FAO.[60] The plant varieties held in these research centres are in the public domain and available without restriction or access fees, but access terms and benefit sharing obligations are regulated by FAO Treaty's multilateral system through standardized material transfer agreements.[61] Since the providing country cannot be identified because of past collection methods, financial benefits accrue to a multilateral trust fund, managed by FAO, for the benefit of the international community, and the purpose of strengthening public sector research on food and agriculture. It is important to note that even this system does not extend to all the genetic material held by these seed banks: the FAO Treaty has adopted a list of plant varieties in an appendix to the Treaty. The appendix does include all the major food crops, which thus become easily available for research towards the FAO objective of food security. This is a centralized system of collective management of genetic resources for the international community that contradicts the idea of genetic gold by retaining elements of a common heritage regime, at least for the specific list of 64 crops.

In a rather bizarre twist in terms of treaty drafting practice, a similar 'global multilateral benefit-sharing mechanism' is *not* actually instituted by the article of the protocol bearing this title.[62] Instead, the 'need and modalities' of such a mechanism covering these different categories of genetic resources are to be further considered by the parties. Where the same resources or traditional knowledge are to be found across the jurisdiction of multiple parties, they are asked to 'endeavour to cooperate, as appropriate...with a view to implementing the Protocol'.[63] The provisions in this area are decidedly weak, and thus the market is decidedly less regulated. Even if instituted, such a global ABS

86 The regulation of genetic gold

mechanism would not be a centralized management system akin to FAO's regime, but would only apply to specific categories of genetic resources not covered by national legislation or bilateral trade agreements.

The protocol appears to mimic arrangements under the FAO treaty. In the FAO system, a central benefit-sharing mechanism is a functional addition because the plant genetic resources under the scope of that system are actually held in the public collections of the global CGIAR network, which is, in turn, controlled by FAO.[64] So there is a conceptual and structural correspondence between a type of global and publicly held resource and its utilization through public, non-commercial R&D. Patents are not granted on products developed based on CGIAR genetic resources. The circumstances of the genetic resources under the scope of the CBD's ABS mechanism are so different – in terms of resource ownership, legal status, and type of research, amongst other factors – as to make a wholesale copying of the regime from one legal context to the other impractical.

Legal effect

The protocol does offer a template ABS process to be followed, seeking harmonization and convergence in the regulation of a new global bioeconomy. It is also a binding legal instrument, yet – in similar fashion to its parent CBD – it is difficult to see how any new legal obligation can be mandated on the basis of this agreement. As expected from international treaty law, rights and obligations from existing international agreements are not to be affected,[65] and no hierarchy is to be created between the protocol and other international agreements.[66] But the legal text includes an additional, strangely insistent, future pre-emption (as if this had to be anxiously spelt out) that 'nothing in the Protocol shall prevent Parties from developing or implementing relevant international agreements, including other specialized access and benefit-sharing agreements'.[67] There is more qualification added in terms of creating exemptions for particular genetic resources: 'where a specialized international access and benefit-sharing instrument applies…this Protocol does not apply to the Party or Parties to the specialized instrument in respect of the specific genetic resource covered by and for the purpose of that special instrument.'[68] The cumulative effect of the provisions that set out the relationship of the protocol with other international instruments can be interpreted as a *de facto no-effect clause*, going to great lengths to make the agreement as formally inconsequential and legally irrelevant as possible. On this basis, the negative assessments coming from the legal field, as outlined in Chapter 1, are therefore not surprising. The formality of a binding protocol to a framework convention is wasted on what amounts to a *de facto* aspirational soft law; after the CBD, there is no law with teeth here either.

If one is to approach the protocol, however, as a governmental programme in response to a problematization of certain legal practices outlined earlier in

The regulation of genetic gold 87

the chapter, then the focus of the assessment, from a governmental perspective, will differ. The emphasis will be less on the form, and more on the substance of the programme. Then the programme will have to contend with a number of biodiversity realities, as presented below.

The weight of genetic gold

The institution and regulation of an as far as possible harmonized and uniform ABS process was, therefore, the legal solution to an unregulated global market created by the genetic gold rush. It was a response to the problematization of the CBD and the regime's practices in terms of benefit redistribution.

The Nagoya protocol instituting this solution took eight years to negotiate, more than the biodiversity convention itself. It thus represents a major attempt of the CBD at maintaining legitimacy, authority, and outright relevancy with the changing conceptions of biodiversity. As stated earlier, it was eventually given a place in the legal structure of the CBD as 'the instrument of implementation of the access and benefit-sharing provisions of the Convention'.[69] Legal issues with the protocol, in terms of its overall questionable legal effect and the bizarre non-negotiation of a global ABS mechanism, were explored at the end of the previous section.

There is another set of broader political issues that are addressed in this section, namely the practices of resource markets such as those envisioned by genetic gold, the relation between ABS and agricultural practices, as well as with the conservation elements of the biodiversity problematization. Above all, however, looms an obvious reality, which is the inevitable end of the genetic gold rush that occurred long before the conclusion of negotiations for the protocol.

Market practices

The genetic resources that were the focus of bioprospecting and consequently were expected to be traded in the presumptive global bioeconomy refer mainly to non-domesticated and non-documented varieties of plants and other organisms located *in situ*, in the last remaining areas of high biodiversity in the Global South. Hence, this is a market for what is termed 'wild' biodiversity.

This market for wild biodiversity transformed into genetic resources was largely dominated by the investment decisions and conduct of private actors of considerable power, such as multinational pharmaceutical corporations and the biotechnology industry. As noted earlier, Merck was essential to the INBio experiment. It was primarily corporate actors, such as Merck, as well as, secondly, various research institutions, universities, their offshoots, and spinoffs that constituted the would-be buyers and 'users' of this wild biodiversity. They would provide the demand for this economy. They undertook commercial and non-commercial (applied and academic) research projects for the

88 The regulation of genetic gold

collection and testing of new biological and/or genetic samples of plants, animals, or other micro-organisms, in search for new profitable natural products. Yet, especially in hindsight, this is and very much always was a niche market, if one removed the rose-tinted development glasses to take proper stock of some market realities.

First, the whole enterprise remains heavily dependent on these private actors to produce economic value, in the specific sense of utilizing these genetic resources for the development of commercial products. But only a limited number of multinational corporations across the world even engaged in such bioprospecting-based research. Warnings about the overall cyclical and unpredictable nature of trends in pharmaceutical research were already observed at the onset of the genetic gold rush.[70] In more recent years, the turn to synthetic biology also reduced the value of 'wild' genetic resources.[71] Furthermore, the chances of developing a viable commercial product were low enough to question the suggestion that bioprospecting would ever scale up to fulfil the great promise of genetic gold. The example of Shaman Pharmaceuticals, the poster child and 'success story' of the genetic gold rush, that spent three decades and a lot of investor funds trying to develop and market a single medicine based on the already well-known traditional and indigenous knowledge of medicinal properties of the red latex sap of the *Croton lechleri* tree should serve as a cautionary tale of the perils of genetic gold.[72]

Second, for the purposes of R&D conducted by the biotechnology industry, a much more accessible raw material are the *ex situ* holdings of documented genetic material that were collected before the entry into force of the biodiversity convention. These collections were located predominantly in the North,[73] under the care of institutions such as botanic gardens, gene banks, etc. Due to past collection methods, most of this genetic material held *ex situ* is of unknown origin, so prior informed consent and benefit-sharing with a providing country or local community cannot be established.[74] Free from the necessity to negotiate access and benefit sharing, these genetic resources are a much more financially attractive solution to bioprospecting, to the extent that resorting to these *ex situ* collections is fast becoming the preferred research practice. This, in effect, circumvents and short-circuits the notion that bioprospecting would ever have reached the volume of traditional agriculture and obviates much of the specialized ABS legislation adopted by the Global South in order to benefit from the genetic gold rush.

Third, the provider of genetic material is still left with the preparatory tasks of the process, such as collection, initial screening, or taxonomy, while the user is tasked with the task of utilization and commercialization that will yield the requisite benefits. This means that the provider still provides the raw material for the user to add economic value through the application of advanced knowledge. Based on standard Lockean conceptions of economic value, the majority of these benefits, at least financially, should accrue to the user that created the added value, as opposed to the provider of the raw material. From this perspective, the differences between the market economy of genetic gold and the agricultural export-oriented model are not as significant as initially advertised. Greater imbalances in terms of techno-science in the world would need to have been addressed for this schema to make sense as an economic development model without colonial undertones.

Finally, in any event there is always the inescapable argument in favour of deregulation. Additional regulation of the sector, such as the one attempted by the Nagoya protocol, would result in the rising costs of securing access permits and certificates of origin and would push these corporations towards different research paths, such as channelling R&D investment towards *ex situ* collections, synthetic biology, and generally anything other than CBD-regulated genetic resources. Adding layers of regulation to a struggling market would be considered problematic for the main corporate drivers of said market.[75]

Ecological effect

Confusion reigns when it comes to the environmental outcomes expected to materialize out of this bioeconomy of genetic gold. This, after all, was the starting point for all this; finding alternative sources of funding for biodiversity conservation. But private ABS arrangements and bioprospecting contracts are, at the very least, unconventional tools of environmental law and policy.[76] They can be classified as incentive mechanisms belonging to the broader category of market-based environmental regulation.[77] There are two main issues with this economic interpretation: first, it is unclear what kind of behaviour is being incentivized and whether it is in fact conducive to biodiversity conservation or even broader environmental goals; second, it is clear from the reality of the market for genetic resources and the quantity and quality of bioprospecting contracts that there isn't significant value in the narrow economic sense for such incentives to materialize. What one ends up with is that 'like so much economic theorizing, the logic is impeccable as long as one buys into the assumptions'.[78]

The terminology employed in the Protocol, derived largely from contract and property law, creates a world of markets, buyers, sellers, and contractual clauses. The connection to the other two objectives of the CBD, i.e., conservation and sustainable use, has grown so distant in the decades of rushing towards genetic gold profits that the protocol includes a tepid reminder in case it has been forgotten that we are still in the realm of biodiversity:

> The Parties shall encourage users and providers to direct benefits arising from the utilization of genetic resources towards the conservation of biological diversity and the sustainable use of its components.[79]

The ABS mechanism is traversed by the logic of the bioprospecting contract, and thus by default ABS arrangements would continue to accrue in areas where there is a better chance of striking 'genetic gold', rather than areas that suffer from environmental degradation. ABS contracts are in essence private arrangements between parties that quite possibly may not be motivated by environmental concerns. The market expects contracts to be negotiated according to economic and not conservation priorities. They would, more often than not, be confined within the national jurisdiction where the access permit is secured. This practice may then constitute an obstacle to any regional environmental conservation initiatives. Lastly, the predictability and flow of any environmental benefit, such as additional conservation funding, is ultimately dependent on negotiating skills in the context of a free market.

Ultimately, a perverse geography is at play when charting the potential direct ecological effect of genetic gold's bioeconomy. It offers little support to wild biodiversity that has been or is in danger of being irrevocably destroyed, but may secure financing to improve some already conserved and managed parts of it. It remains unclear why a system of focusing exclusively on the limited number of areas of high biodiversity should be translated into environmental policy for the very diverse whole.

At its most pragmatic, as an expression of environmental economics, genetic gold could thus be positioned as an innovative mechanism that further consolidates the restructuring of conservation finance abandoning the model of development assistance from the North to the South and adopting market-based approaches.[80] However, the location and type of beneficiaries offer only indirect and hazily understood benefits in terms of environmental protection and biodiversity conservation. It remains unclear whether these ABS arrangements are supposed to procure funding predominantly for the environment or for development, once outside the facile closure of the assumptions underpinning sustainable development.

Knowledge practices

The Nagoya protocol, in addition to its inability to take into account market and environmental realities surrounding the practice it was attempting to regulate, also had further unintended effects that compounded its negative reception. Another long-standing concern mishandled by the protocol was the clarification of distinct access and benefit sharing requirements for academic and applied research.[81]

The ABS acronym, like its associated bioprospecting label, can serve to make such distinctions in research unclear, and to homogenize the varied, academic, and commercial, purposes for sample collection and genetic research. The multiplying joint ventures and links between business and academia further blur the lines between the two types of research. Nevertheless, there is a dividing line that is possible to discern. It is obvious that success in bioprospecting is not measured in the same way in the academic and applied fields. For academic research programmes, success is measured primarily in terms of building

The regulation of genetic gold 91

knowledge on life, what has been termed *biodiscovery*, or at least increasing taxonomic precision. Industrial or commercial programmes aim to develop marketable products, in the form of new natural products, pharmaceuticals and/or crop varieties; i.e., to 'commercialize' biodiversity. Different criteria for success also bring different types and levels of funding. Applied research is privately funded by large multinational corporations, while academic research has to rely, at least to a certain extent, on some form of public funding or grant.

Despite such obvious differences, the Protocol continues to regard the ABS mechanism as equally applicable to all types of biodiversity research. The only ground ceded is the restatement of the principle that ABS legislation is not meant to fence off and block access to genetic resources, but to promote research and development, especially of the type that contributes to the other two objectives of the CBD (conservation and sustainable use).[82] However, there is no specific allowance made for academic research to be subject to simplified measures compared to commercial R&D. Given the discrepancy in financial resources and the differing objectives, excessively onerous access requirements will invariably continue to stifle any form of non-commercial and public good-oriented research that is not native to the market economy of genetic gold. And given how the latter has turned out, such regulations will affect academic, much more than they will commercial, research.

The end of genetic gold

The more important question, however, is whether the response was appropriate to the scale of the problem or even relevant to an actually existing phenomenon or problem. By the time the protocol was adopted, let alone entered into force, the genetic gold rush had long gone, and the bubble had burst.[83] Bioprospecting and ABS arrangements never reached sufficient mass to support this envisaged bioeconomy. The life sciences moved from Eisner's natural product discovery to synthetic biology. For these genetic resources to act as a source of significant benefits and sustained income for the providers of genetic material, bioprospecting programmes and ABS arrangements had to attain an unreal level of success; predictably, that level simply never materialized.[84] The conceptual weight that was placed on genetic resources was too much to bear.

Doubts were expressed about the viability of emerging markets for genetic resources as early as in 1988, even before genetic gold was disseminated as a win-win scenario of environmental management for the South.[85] But a gold rush remains a rush, irrespective of the nature of the green gold. To a certain extent, therefore, the protocol, with all its compromises and issues, was an international legal response to a problem that was no longer present. The regulatory framework was obsolete in the very moment it was agreed. A number of issues emerged from this chronological disjunction.

ABS arrangements are not simple contracts for the procurement of genetic material, and the bioeconomy was not simply another economic venture or alternative development model. They were instead loaded with expectations from the start; hybrid public/private arrangements hitting upon a multiplicity of social, economic, political, and environmental issues, in addition to having to make some form of business sense and atone for past (failed) development ideologies and environmental policies. The weight of expectations placed a significant burden on these agreements, to deliver on multiple levels. The CBD clearly did not lift this burden with the Nagoya protocol. But then, in a certain sense, it is the weight of genetic gold that dragged everything down. This was a rationality built on an underlying resource that ultimately could not carry it.

The ABS mechanism, if interpreted as a programme of government responding to the genetic gold problematization, is focused on the micro level of bringing together, through a market transaction, a producer and a buyer (in the convention's discourse a provider and a user) of a certain product (in this case the raw material of genetic resources). This exchange would be facilitated and supported by increasing the documentation, indexing, commodification, and commercialization of these resources, by increasing a particular kind of biodiversity knowledge. If the ABS mechanism is then to be understood differently, it should not be by reference to international law and grand North–South bargains; it is a more intimate technology geared towards arranging the details of this coming together so as to produce the desired effects. In this guise, its primary goal is to produce the human subject of the provider/seller of genetic resources, a subject capable of navigating this new reality for their benefit.[86]

The biodiversity convention started life as a conservation instrument and then became an instrument of sustainable development. In a move echoing this evolution, the Nagoya protocol started life as an instrument creating a new centralized institution, before becoming a form of voluntary market regulation, aiming for harmonization in similar fashion to the Bonn guidelines and other regional initiatives. Neither agreement is presently close to its conceptual origins.

Notes

1 William Gibson, *Zero History* (2010).
2 Or *living modified organisms (LMOs)* in the language of the CBD. See CBD, Art. 19(3), which explicitly envisages the adoption of the Cartagena Protocol on Biosafety (1999)
3 For example, see COP Decision II/12 (1995), which dealt solely with intellectual property rights and their impact on biodiversity conservation, without reference to access to genetic resources or benefit-sharing.
4 Mainly expressed though the – then – newly formed negotiating Group of 77 (G77) and China, also active in the context of WTO negotiations. See CBD, *Report of the Second Meeting of COP to the CBD* (UN Doc. UNEP/CBD/COP/2/19, 1995), par. 107.
5 Jakarta Ministerial Declaration on the Implementation of the CBD (UN Doc. UNEP/CBD/COP/2/19, 1995), Appendix, par. 5.

The regulation of genetic gold 93

6 CBD, Art. 3.
7 For a detailed exploration of the concept beyond the legal/political field of this research see Anna Deplazes-Zemp, '"Genetic Resourses": An Analysis of a Multi-Faceted Concept' (2018) 222 *Biological Conservation* 86.
8 Kerry ten Kate, 'Science and the Convention on Biological Diversity' (2002) 295 *Science* 2371, 2371.
9 CBD, Art. 15(2): 'Each Contracting Party shall endeavour to create conditions to facilitate access to genetic resources...and not to impose restrictions that run counter to the objectives of the Convention.'
10 Andean Pact, Decision 391, *Common Regime on Access to Genetic Resources* (1996). The decision instituted minimum rules to be applied by all member states of the pact. Available at: https://www.wipo.int/edocs/lexdocs/laws/en/bo/bo012en.pdf.
11 *African Model Law for the Protection of the Rights of Local Communities, Farmers and Breeders, and for the Regulation of Access to Biological Resources* (2000) by the (then Organization of African Unity) African Union. Available at: https://www.wipo.int/edocs/lexdocs/laws/en/oau/oau001en.pdf.
12 Cabrera, Jorge and Garforth, Kathryn, 'Global Access, Local Benefits: An International Access and Benefit Sharing Regime?' in Cordonier Segger, M C and Weeramantry, C G (eds), *Sustainable Justice: Reconciling Economic, Social and Environmental Law* (Martinus Nijhoff Publishers, Leiden; Boston, 2005) 223.
13 Timo Goeschl and others, 'Incentivizing Ecological Destruction? The Global Joint Regulation of the Conservation and Use of Genetic Resources' (2005) 38 *Ind L Rev* 619.
14 Shamama Afreen and Biju Paul Abraham, 'Bioprospecting: Promoting and Regulating Access to Genetic Resources and Benefit Sharing' (2009) 36 *Decision* 121.
15 As recounted in Chapter 4 *supra*.
16 Vandana Shiva, *Monocultures of the Mind: Perspectives on Biodiversity and Biotechnology* (Zed Books 1993) 151.
17 COP Decision VI/24 (2002), Annex. [Bonn guidelines].
18 I.e., containing functional units of heredity as defined in CBD, Art. 2
19 I.e., biochemicals.
20 For more information on the additions to standard CBD 'doctrine' see Stephen Tully, 'The Bonn Guidelines on Access to Genetic Resources and Benefit Sharing' (2003) 12 *Review of European Community and International Environmental Law* 84 86.
21 These were outlined in Bonn Guidelines, Art. 42(b)(iv).
22 COP Decision VII/19 (2004), Art. 1.
23 CBD, Art. 2.
24 Ibid.
25 Ibid.
26 The CBD only included a definition of the broader term 'sustainable use', which was essentially an adjustment of the sustainability/sustainable development definition of the 1987 Brundtland Report. See CBD, Art. 2: '"Sustainable use" means the use of components of biological diversity in a way and at a rate that does not lead to the long-term decline of biological diversity, thereby maintaining its potential to meet the needs and aspirations of present and future generations.'
27 CBD, Art. 15.3, 15.7. Protocol, Art. 5.
28 CBD, Art. 2. Protocol, Art. 2.
29 Protocol, Art. 5.
30 CBD, Art. 8(j).
31 Protocol, Art. 5.2.
32 Protocol, Art. 5.5.
33 Protocol, Art. 6.2.

94 The regulation of genetic gold

34 Protocol, Art. 6.3(f).
35 Protocol, Art. 7.
36 Protocol, Art. 12.3.
37 Protocol, Art. 12.1.
38 Protocol, Art. 6.1.
39 Protocol, Art. 6.3(b).
40 Protocol, Art. 6.3(d).
41 Protocol, Art. 5.1.
42 Protocol, Art. 15.1.
43 Lyle Glowka, 'Emerging Legislative Approaches to Implement Article 15 of the Convention on Biological Diversity' (1997) 6 *Review of European Community and International Environmental Law* 249 257; R.V. Anuradha, 'In Search of Knowledge and Resources: Who Sows? Who Reaps?' (1997) 6 *Review of European Community and International Environmental Law* 263.
44 Protocol, Art. 6.2.
45 Protocol, Art. 6.3(f).
46 Protocol, Art. 5.1. These terms should be agreed in writing before the access permit is granted. An indicative list of such terms is included in Art. 6.3(g).
47 Protocol, Art. 5.4.
48 Ibid.
49 Marie Bystrom and others, *Fair and Equitable: Sharing the Benefits from Use of Genetic Resources and Traditional Knowledge*, 1999).
50 Bonn guidelines, Art 45.
51 CBD, *Report of the Panel of Experts on Access and Benefit Sharing on the Work of its Second Meeting* (UN Doc UNEP/CBD/WG-ABS/1/2, 2001), par. 47, 112.
52 UNEP/CBD/COP Decision VII.19 (2004), Annex.
53 Protocol, Art. 6.3(e) and 14.
54 Protocol, Art. 17(2).
55 Protocol, Art. 17.
56 Protocol, Art. 17.1(a)(ii).
57 Protocol, Art. 17.1(a)(iv).
58 Protocol, Art. 16.2.
59 CGIAR holds 12% of the world's collected genetic material.
60 See International Treaty on Plant Genetic Resources for Food and Agriculture (FAO Treaty).
61 FAO Treaty, Arts. 10–13, 15–16.
62 Protocol, Art. 10.
63 Protocol, Art. 11
64 The FAO system is also helped in its operation by its reduced complexity due to limited scope. There is a list of specific plant varieties for food and agriculture that are managed through the system.
65 Protocol, Art. 4.1.
66 Protocol, Ibid.
67 Art. 4.2.
68 Protocol, Art 4.4.
69 Protocol, Art. 4.4.
70 ten Kate (n.8); Walter V. Reid and others, *Biodiversity Prospecting: Using Genetic Resources for Sustainable Development* (World Resources Institute, USA 1993), 15 ff.
71 Sarah A Laird and Rachel Wynberg, *Bioscience at a Crossroads: Implementing the Nagoya Protocol on Access and Benefit Sharing in a Time of Scientific, Technological and Industry Change* (Secretariat of the Convention on Biological Diversity, 2012).

The regulation of genetic gold 95

72 Roger Alex Clapp and Carolyn Crook, 'Drowning in the Magic Well: Shaman Pharmaceuticals and the Elusive Value of Traditional Knowledge' (2002) 11 *Journal of Environment & Development* 79.

73 An actual 75% of genetic material held in *ex situ* collections is located in either the US or Europe. Tully (n.20), 97.

74 In fact, only 25% of the genetic material collected before the entry into force of the CBD is of known origin. Ibid.

75 Laird and Wynberg (n.71).

76 For example, they are not mentioned at all in the nomenclature of available market-based environmental measures in Daniel Bodansky, *The Art and Craft of International Environmental Law* (Harvard University Press 2010) 57–85.

77 Joseph Henry Vogel, 'From the "Tragedy of the Commons" to the "Tragedy of the Commonplace": Analysis and Synthesis through the Lens of Economic Theory' in Charles R. McManis (ed), *Biodiversity and the Law : Intellectual Property, Biotechnology & Traditional Knowledge* (Earthscan 2007).

78 Ibid, 121.

79 Protocol, Art. 9.

80 As explained in the previous chapter.

81 Sylvia I Martinez and Susette Biber-Klemm, 'Scientists – Take Action for Access to Biodiversity' (2010) 2 *Current Opinion in Environmental Sustainability* 27.

82 Protocol, Art. 8(a).

83 Laird and Wynberg.

84 James S. Miller, 'Impact of the Convention on Biological Diversity: The Lessons from Ten Years of Experience with Models of Equitable Sharing of Benefits' in Charles R. McManis (ed), *Biodiversity and the Law: Intellectual Property, Biotechnology and Traditional Knowledge* (Earthscan 2007).

85 See reservations already expressed in David Ehrenfeld, 'Why Put a Value on Biodiversity?" in Edward O. Wilson (ed), *Biodiversity* (National Academy Press 1988).

86 This process is further analyzed in Andreas Kotsakis, 'Change and Subjectivity in International Environmental Law: The Micro-Politics of the Transformation of Biodiversity into Genetic Gold' (2014) 3 *TEL* 127.

Conclusion
Still here

The genealogist will know what to make of this masquerade. He will not be too serious to enjoy it; on the contrary, he will push the masquerade to its limit and prepare the great carnival of time where masks are constantly reappearing.[1]

In the case of biodiversity, it was not a child that exposed the emperor's new clothes, but conservationists and practitioners operating on the ground and away from the international law and policy fora where biodiversity was celebrated. As early as 1997, RA Lautenschlager, an Ontario conservationist, published a short piece in the *Wildlife Society Bulletin* excoriating the still very popular biodiversity, which 'was so all-inclusive that it has become meaningless'.[2] Biodiversity's general definition as some form of variety or diversity of life 'fails to provide understanding when used in communications for research or management'.[3] Without a more clearly stated definition, and crucially some way to organize priorities, biodiversity could not provide actual guidance for decisions. It signified 'little more than "feel-good" meaning'.[4] In genealogical terms, therefore, his argument was that biodiversity had not been sufficiently or correctly governmentalized, i.e., problematized and thought of as an object of government.

Enhancing and maintaining diversity in the abstract was not an effective programme for redrawing conservation practices or managing ecosystems. The counter argument is that the generality and vagueness of the general good of biodiversity was replaced with concrete targets and metrics;[5] for example, the percentage of land designated as a protected area. The Aichi targets were a first detailed manifestation of such a programme in the context of the biodiversity convention. However, global or national land designations of protected areas did not appreciably reduce the abstraction or add any significant insight into how these lands were to be managed. The appearance of a number or statistic by itself is insufficient to increase precision, and these targets only served to accentuate the theme of broad scope and non-existent instruments that characterized the biodiversity convention from the start.

What about 'sustainable utilization'? Here, the story has not been that different. Bioprospecting did not work either, genetic gold never reaching

Conclusion   97

critical mass before the biotechnology industry moved on to other forms of raw material for biodiscovery and research and development. The genetic gold boom gave way to bust, the vision of a future bioeconomy strongly muted, although renewed infatuations with the life sciences periodically bring back some notion of combining biology and economics in a series of 'bioconcepts'.[6] The centrality of biodiversity as genetic resources in such a bioeconomy is not a formulation that any governmental thought will return to anytime soon.

Biodiversity has not been conserved effectively or used sustainably under the biodiversity convention's watch. Given such dismal outcomes, it is not difficult to understand how the perception of failure swirls around biodiversity itself as a concept, as well as its primary international instrument tasked with protecting the essential infrastructure of all life on Earth, with ensuring the protection of 'the life sustaining systems of the biosphere'.[7] The 'tide of loss' has continued for decades, leading to negativity towards biodiversity, which has fallen out of academic and policy vogue.[8] Global biodiversity's 'grand bargain' fell into irrelevance, as globalization itself waned. Conservation funding (or finance if you prefer) is still lacking today, and the genetic gold rush was unable to affect the trend. Biodiversity 'reserves' have continued to dwindle, and their decline across the world remains a serious environmental problem. An age of extinction remains firmly upon us.

Despite all this, the biodiversity convention is still here. It persists, preparing for its third strategic plan, and entering its fourth decade of operation. It is far from a sleeping treaty, but is rather an undead convention: a sprawling edifice and a major node in the group of biodiversity-related conventions, the global biodiversity regime.[9] This realization – and it may well be a realization in various quarters of environmental law scholarship content with the notion that biodiversity is just another, more scientific-sounding, word for nature – calls for distinctions between the genetic gold rush of the 1990s, another type of exuberant bubble and buzzword that fizzled out, the regime's earlier descent from within conservation biology, its internationalization as part of a grand bargain, and its contemporary present. The conservation perspective, the grand bargain, and genetic gold programmes had their time, and their failures dragged the biodiversity convention into obscurity; it is now the backwater from where this book's investigation commenced.

The explanation that this book offers to the question of the regime's persistence is rather direct: neither biodiversity itself nor the convention is what we traditionally think them to be on the basis of mainstream legal interpretations. What international law sees is a failing convention shuffling on; what legal academia sees is a research interest that has had its time. Both have, largely, moved on.

Findings of the legal genealogy

The genealogical approach adopted for this book instead excavates, and captures, an environmental reason – biodiversity as a form of thought that

98 Conclusion

underlies and structures the convention. Based on the suspicion and hypothesis that the biodiversity convention is not simply another international agreement and that biodiversity represents far more than a technical environmental problem of conservation, the book provides an account of a series of problematizations, practices, and programmes. It uses the analytical units of problems and responses/solutions to these problems, as opposed to relying on traditional categories of legal analysis, such as institutions, principles, and obligations.

This legal genealogy demonstrated how a number of different objects and practices became conceived of as problems of government, i.e., were problematized and ultimately governmentalized, under the ostensible banners of biological diversity, biodiversity, global biodiversity, and the like. Conservation practices, environmental advocacy, human population and society, conservation funding, the Global South, development, domestic environmental laws, or international environmental law itself (among other practices) were at times the targets of a problematization organized under the umbrella term and branded with the label of biodiversity. As a result, the proposals for action, that is, the programmes of government put forward in response to these problematizations, were equally varied, but carefully nestled under the same umbrella. There is thus significant diversity in biodiversity thought, even more so than depicted in the pages of this book. This is far from a comprehensive intellectual history of biodiversity, just a snapshot related to the notion of genetic gold.

This demonstration went further than simply establishing biodiversity's contingency, i.e., the already accepted understanding that, much like sustainable development, biodiversity has meant different things to different people and social groups at different times. Such malleability, bordering on incoherence, of vision has often been the target of criticism, and the outcomes of the Nagoya conference are no exception to this tendency, as outlined in Chapter 1. Instead, this genealogy focused on showing how biodiversity's conceptions have been put to use in pursuit of governmental programmes that are as varied, heterogeneous, and dynamic (despite their organization under the biodiversity label) as the problematizations from which they are derived. Environmental and conservation concerns form a part of this process, but they are not always at the centre.

This particular methodology was also chosen to counteract the conceptual manoeuvre whereby international environmental law, in general, as well as the biodiversity convention, use history as a source of legitimacy in two, seemingly contrasting, ways. On the one hand, environmental law is often seen as ahistorical; a recent set of principles and norms that shape humanity's response to an urgent crisis.[10] Their legitimacy is thus derived from their urgency, the alarm over the future, and the absence of a history. On the other hand, international environmental law derives its legitimacy from a particular progressive legal historical teleology, structured around specific seminal events, in the shape of international conferences, often beginning with the 1972 Stockholm UN Conference on the Human Environment.[11]

The genealogy completed here did not locate a single origin for creating a singular, complete, or final conception of biodiversity or its convention, but a set of problems that attached themselves to the vehicle of biodiversity and international environmental law at different times over the last decades, altering the direction of travel. Neither the meaning nor the applications of the idea of biodiversity are fixed, but have been constantly problematized since its introduction in a variety of ways. In other words, that there is no single global biodiversity crisis, but a contingent composition of divergent problematizations that shifted over certain periods, often presenting themselves as a crisis – in terms of conservation, environmental protection, development, the political economy of the Global South, etc.

From this genealogical perspective, therefore, the convention itself started life as one such programme, a response to the problematization of the absence of international cooperation to address a global threat of species extinction and biodiversity loss. But even in its beginnings, it appeared to go in a different direction. Eschewing the introduction of new legal principles and obligations for state parties, it appeared to scholars as quasi-soft law from the start,[12] an understanding only confirmed by the most recent Nagoya Protocol.[13] There were no significant challenges with implementation as there were no distinctions between lawful and unlawful action in relation to the specific environmental problem at hand. The difference with other biodiversity-related treaties is significant. For example, CITES[14] concentrates on the regulation of wildlife trade and wants to isolate and prevent its more destructive manifestations by establishing the illegality of trade in a number of globally listed endangered animals. A rule breach in such regimes is easy to identify based on their system of prohibition; if certain wild animals are still traded, there is a violation. For biodiversity, treaty violations do not exist and have never existed, unless one counts submitting national biodiversity action plans late.

This classical framing of an environmental problem in need of intervention from the international community was swiftly upended by its encounter with sustainable development, and then by the Global South's own problematizations of biodiversity in the context of resource distribution. Genetic gold 'fever' completed the shift. Then the issue became the management of present realities in terms of people and resources, and not some future where biodiversity loss will have been arrested. Throughout the genetic gold rush and ultimately the attempt to respond to its problematization from within, through the Nagoya protocol, the biodiversity regime veered further and further away from conservation practice and classical environmental law in the service of ecological goals, towards finding ways to make correct use of biodiversity as a resource to support human society. The practice was no longer nature viewed through the lens of biodiversity, as promoted by conservation biology, but a society (and economy) arranged through the lens of biodiversity; social systems viewed in conjunction with the ecosystems of biodiversity.

A technology and a laboratory

From the particular genealogical perspective employed here, therefore, biodiversity is neither an idea nor a representation of an environmental reality. It is instead a device, a political technology, through which governing is imagined and made possible. Biodiversity is thus a technology of government, i.e., a tool that allows the framing of governmental thought, of an argument regarding what 'needs to be done' or rather what needs to be governed (and how). This line of thought can be defined as biodiversity reason. If one were to push this argument further, we can posit biodiversity as a tool for governing people. The biopolitical implications of such a claim will have to remain the topic of a different study. Biodiversity reason is still with us today, an underlying grid of rationality, irrespective of whether biodiversity, genetic gold, ecosystem services, or even 'nature's contributions to people' become the academic or policy buzzword of the day.

Consequently, the biodiversity regime is not simply a global regime in response to a global crisis, but something continuously made and unmade to fit political, economic, and scientific paradigm shifts; a laboratory for developing new forms of reason using the technology of biodiversity. It thus has a practical utility and function, in addition to any global symbolism. The regime assumes a primary function as a laboratory for the production of governmental thought, a diffuse and diversified platform where governmental rationalities are developed with the use of the technology of biodiversity. This governmental operation can be distinguished from the operation envisaged by the legal text, as an instrument of international cooperation for the purpose of environmental protection in the area of biodiversity.

This is the core of the explanation of the paradox of the undead convention. The regime was able to keep going and shuffle on because of this underlying format as a laboratory and testing platform. An example of this operation is the prominently billed Nagoya protocol, which is only indirectly driven by environmental concerns, as demonstrated in chapter 6. This protocol sees its parent regime as a *de facto* regulator, attempting to achieve goals related to market regulation, such as regulatory convergence and harmonization. This leads to us to an additional, rather simple realization: the biodiversity convention itself is not a solution, but a platform for solutions. It is not an instrument or a 'weapon' by itself in the fight against biodiversity decline, but the laboratory for developing instruments that make productive use of this phenomenon. This distinction of function and role goes a long way towards explaining its persistence.

It may be comforting for some in the legal discipline to have law as a fixed anchor and steady fort against the hovering maelstrom of contested environmental ethics and politics, and international law is particularly well suited to such an elevation of formal law into universal principles and binding commitments. From a single, overarching, and universal goal of addressing biodiversity loss, authority, and legitimacy flow. The genealogy of the biodiversity convention presented in this book, however, is one filled with 'messy' conflicts, strategies, policies, mechanisms, aspirations, markets, and contracts.

This may seem defeatist, accepting a 'lesser' role for the treaty. The aspirations of international environmental law never materialized. The regime never morphed into an international instrument promoting and enforcing large-scale conservation programmes, based on detailed ecological metrics, standards, and ethics. It is further from such an arrangement now compared to the day it was agreed. It seems more apposite to suggest that the goal is now the improvement of society through the correct use of biodiversity; the urgency of the laboratory's work is not derived from a global biodiversity crisis, but rather from the lack of (sustainable) development or, indeed, economic health. As Cristiana Pasça Palmer, the now disgraced former Executive Secretary, explained in an illuminating fashion in 2019:

> It is not 'saving the planet' that will kill growth. Rather, the accelerating destruction of nature will undermine not only the global economy, but it could eventually threaten many life-forms on earth, including our own species…The fundamental question is thus how to save the planet, and the economy with it, from this generations-long crisis.[15]

Thus, saving biodiversity matters in the context of saving the global economy. The environmental crisis has been submerged within a global economic crisis.

The rise of the Intergovernmental Science–Policy Platform on Biodiversity and Ecosystem Services (IPBES) as the premier global instrument of biodiversity knowledge production[16] has implications for this conception of the biodiversity convention as a laboratory. IPBES belongs to the growing matrix of science policy interfaces or transnational regulatory scientific institutions now playing a prominent role in global environmental governance.[17] It was established in 2012,[18] as an intergovernmental body open to all UN member states, to meet a knowledge gap in biodiversity assessment[19] and constitute a 'communication node' between biodiversity science and policy.[20] This positioning led to its catchy moniker of 'IPCC for biodiversity', but there is divergence from that model[21] by adding knowledge production, capacity building, and policy support functions to its programme of operation.[22] As expected from similar science–policy platforms, IPBES outputs should be 'policy relevant, but not policy prescriptive'.[23]

According to the mainstream history of IPBES, the necessity for such a knowledge institution was precipitated by the inability of the biodiversity convention's own scientific advisory body (the SBSTTA) to overcome its politicization along state lines and 'function as an independent scientific unit',[24] while at the same time independent scientific assessments that did not proceed through some form of international state cooperation were equally not accepted by states. This explains the hybrid legal form of such regulatory science institutions, which combine both intergovernmental and science panel aspects.

102   Conclusion

Although IPBES may thus appear as a complementary or at least corrective institution for the global biodiversity regime, it can also be interpreted as a direct challenge to the biodiversity convention. If the biodiversity convention is, as the genealogical analysis demonstrates, itself a testing platform and a laboratory for developing technologies of government on the basis of varied problematizations of biodiversity, would then a purpose-built, better 'equipped' platform and laboratory not be a significant improvement? IPBES's complex structure, incorporating input from experts from across academic disciplines, international organizations, and states,[25] appears to provide such a laboratory.

The possibility of the convention being rendered *de facto* obsolete is further supported by a comparison of the substantive output and policy impact of the two institutions. As the epigraph in the very beginning of this book intimates, biodiversity (and its grand bargain and genetic gold notions) have *de facto* been replaced in the environmental imagination by ecosystem services, a broader and different and broader economic conception of nature and biodiversity.[26] The details and merits of this transformation escape the present work, and have been examined elsewhere.[27] What matters for the purposes of this comparison is where this innovation took place. Which of the two competing laboratories is regarded as the innovator that brought and applied this new technology of valuing nature? The answer is in the IPBES acronym itself. It would have been a great achievement for the biodiversity convention, irrespective of the assessment of the effects of ecosystem services,[28] if this new programme emerged from the laboratory of the biodiversity regime. Therefore, IPBES represents a direct challenge to the future of the biodiversity convention. Anything that the latter can do as a platform, the former can also do in a more purpose-built and organized manner.

Direction of travel

The convention thus signifies a point where international environmental law ceases to be the exclusive space of the scientist, the economist, the diplomat, the environmental lawyer, or, indeed, the environmental activist and the alliances forged between them. Legal principles and obligations, the pragmatism of economics, the ecological truth of the global biodiversity crisis, the North–South grand bargain are not enough in isolation to establish the goals and provide an evaluative schema of the regime. Biodiversity has travelled far from the traditional borders of international environmental law, and into uncharted territory. It has done so without a lot of equipment, in terms of power or authority, but it has proven a certain capacity for survival and adaptation, much like the species it once thought it was going to protect.

The fact that the convention was not drafted or designed in the manner in which it currently operates should not be a crucial element in its assessment. Its origin as an international treaty or conservation instrument does not hold some form of sacred truth about its environmentalist essence, which is being lost by its contemporary focus and operation. Under the influence of the law of treaties, the search for authority always leads back to the legal text in order to define an internal legal rationality of principles and obligations for interpreting and implementing the stated and agreed treaty objectives. While this is where this book started from, it is not where it ends.

With the assistance of genealogy, the established historical narrative of the biodiversity convention, and the regime that is emerging from it, is disrupted and 'pluralized'.[29] The findings seek to reduce the tendency to read the past as a necessary step towards the establishment of the inevitable character of the present, leading to *post facto* rationalizations of events and decisions – a tendency reinforced by the precedent-like character of legal history. The overall effect of this genealogy is 'anti-anachronistic',[30] making restorative forays into legal nostalgia impotent. We cannot use the original treaty to restore belief or commitment to biodiversity.

Consequently, there is no way to evaluate the biodiversity convention by hypothesizing or forcing upon it precisely such external, universal, or distinctly legal or ecological goals that are not immanent to its reason. The realization that the convention does not constitute classical or – even recognizable for some – international environmental law has often been met with disappointment, taken to mean that it constitutes ineffective or disappointing international law that has failed in its primary aim of arresting biodiversity loss. The convention is criticized for not accomplishing enough for environmental protection, for not coming close to securing a future when biodiversity loss will have been eliminated. Instead, we reach the conclusion that the convention is actually neither a failure nor a success as environmental law, because, as this book establishes, it operates differently than a standard environmental treaty regime.

We thus find ourselves, at the end of all this, without the protective anchors of either law or ecology. The regime is, indeed, useful for governmental ends. But genealogy has left us with no way to formally evaluate it by either environmental or legal standards. From where will legitimacy and effectiveness be derived then? This will be the question of forthcoming studies.

Notes

1 Michel Foucault, 'Nietzsche, Genealogy, History' in Paul Rabinow (ed), *The Foucault Reader: An Introduction to Foucault's Thought* (Penguin 1991), 94.
2 R.A. Lautenschlager, 'Biodiversity is Dead' (1997) 25 *Wildlife Society Bulletin* 679.
3 Ibid, 679.
4 Ibid, 683.
5 Esther Turnhout and others, '"Measurementality" in Biodiversity Governance: Knowledge, Transparency, and the Intergovernmental Science-Policy Platform on Biodiversity and Ecosystem Services (IPBES)' (2014) 46 *Environment and Planning A: Economy and Space* 581; Frank Biermann and others, 'Global Governance by

104 Conclusion

Goal-Setting: The Novel Approach of the UN Sustainable Development Goals' (2017) 26–7 *Current Opinion in Environmental Sustainability* 26.

6 Kean Birch and David Tyfield, 'Theorizing the Bioeconomy: Biovalue, Biocapital, Bioeconomics or … What?' (2012) 38 *Science, Technology, & Human Values* 299.

7 CBD, Preamble.

8 Jessica Dempsey, *Enterprising Nature: Economics, Markets, and Finance in Global Biodiversity Politics* (Wiley Blackwell 2016), 1–4.

9 Veit Koester, 'The Five Global Biodiversity-Related Conventions: A Stocktaking' (2002) 11 *Review of European Community and International Environmental Law* 96; Aðalheiður Jóhannsdóttir and others, 'The Current Framework for International Governance: Is it Doing More Harm than Good?' (2010) 19 *Review of European Community and International Environmental Law* 139.

10 On the relation between historical analysis and environmental law (or the absence thereof) see David B. Schorr, 'Historical Analysis in Environmental Law' in Markus B. Dubber and Cristopher Tomlins (eds), *The Oxford Handbook of Legal History* (Oxford University Press 2018).

11 On the historical evolution of international environmental law see Edith Brown Weiss, 'International Environmental Law: Contemporary Issues and the Emergence of a New World Order' (1993) 81 *Geo LJ* 675; Peter H. Sand, 'The Evolution of International Environmental Law' in Daniel Bodansky and others (eds), *The Oxford Handbook of International Environmental Law* (OUP 2007).

12 Such an interpretation is proposed in Alan E. Boyle, 'The Rio Convention on Biological Diversity' in Catherine Redgwell and Michael Bowman (eds), *International Law and the Conservation of Biological Diversity* (Kluwer Law International 1995); Alan E. Boyle, 'Soft Law in International Law-Making' in Malcolm D. Evans (ed), *International Law* (5th edn, Oxford University Press 2018).

13 Stuart R. Harrop and Diana J. Pritchard, 'A Hard Instrument Goes Soft: The Implications of the Convention on Biological Diversity's Current Trajectory' (2011) 21 *Global Environmental Change* 474.

14 *Convention on International Trade in Endangered Species of Wild Fauna and Flora* (1973), 993 U.N.T.S. 243.

15 This was part of a speech given at the World Economic Forum annual meeting in early 2019. Available at: https://www.weforum.org/agenda/2019/01/save-the-pl anet-save-the-economy-cristiana-pasca-palmer/.

16 On this emergence see Alice Vadrot, *The Politics of Knowledge and Global Biodiversity* (Routledge 2014); Thomas M. Brooks and others, 'IPBES ≠ IPCC' (2014) 29 *Trends in Ecology & Evolution* 543.

17 Oren Perez, 'The Hybrid Legal-Scientific Dynamic of Transnational Scientific Institutions' (2015) 26 *EJIL* 391; Adi Ayal and others, 'Science, Politics and Transnational Regulation: Regulatory Scientific Institutions and the Dilemmas of Hybrid Authority' (2013) 2 *TEL* 45.

18 For a historical account of its negotiation and establishment see Leslie-Anne Duvic-Paoli, 'The Intergovernmental Science-Policy Platform for Biodiversity and Ecosystem Services or the Framing of Scientific Knowledge within the Law of Sustainable Development' (2017) 19 *ICLR* 231. To underline its sustainable development roots, IPBES was also acknowledged in the Rio+20 Declaration, see UNGA Res. 66/228 (2012), 'The Future We Want', par. 204.

19 UNEP recognized that 'there are gaps in our knowledge of the state of the environment resulting from a lack of current data and information generation and dissemination', as well as 'the potential benefits of a scientifically sound and evidence-based detailed assessment of the state of the environment for awareness-raising, informed policy formulation and decision-making in the context of sustainable development'. See

UNEA Resolution 1/4 (2014) 'Science-Policy Interface', Preamble. See also UNEP/ IPBES/2/INF/1 (2009), 'Gap Analysis for the Purpose of Facilitating the Discussions on How to Improve and Strengthen the Science-Policy Interface on Biodiversity and Ecosystem Services'.

20 Christoph Görg and others, 'A New Link Between Biodiversity Science and Policy' (2010) 19 *GAIA – Ecological Perspectives for Science and Society* 183.

21 Editorial, 'Wanted: an IPCC for biodiversity' (2010) 465 *Nature* 525; Anne Larigauderie and Harold A. Mooney, 'The Intergovernmental Science-Policy Platform on Biodiversity and Ecosystem Services: Moving a Step Closer to an IPCC-like Mechanism for Biodiversity' (2010) 2 *Current Opinion in Environmental Sustainability* 9. On the different functions of IPBES compared to the IPCC model, see Brooks and others.

22 See Decision IPBES-2/5: Work programme for the period 2014–2018, Annex I for a list of the functions of the platform.

23 Vadrot; Görg and others (n.20).

24 Görg and others (n.20), 183.

25 IPBES, 'Functions, operating principles and institutional arrangements of the Intergovernmental Science-Policy Platform on Biodiversity and Ecosystem Services' (2012).

26 Christian Pip, 'The Convention on Biological Diversity as a Legal Framework for Safeguarding Ecosystem Services' (2018) 29 *Ecosystem Services* 199.

27 Dempsey (n.8).

28 It is worthwhile to note here that IPBES itself is already positing a paradigm shift away from ecosystem services and towards a new term of 'nature's contributions to people'. Garry D. Peterson and others, 'Welcoming different perspectives in IPBES: "Nature's contributions to people" and "Ecosystem services"' (2018) 23 *Ecology and Society* 39; Unai Pascual and others, 'Valuing Nature's Contributions to People: the IPBES Approach' (2017) 26–7 *Current Opinion in Environmental Sustainability* 7; Sandra Díaz and others, 'The IPBES Conceptual Framework: Connecting Nature and People' (2015) 14 *Current Opinion in Environmental Sustainability* 1.

29 Ben Golder, 'Contemporary Legal Genealogies' in Justin Desautels-Stein and Cristopher Tomlins (eds), *Searching for Contemporary Legal Thought* (Cambridge University Press 2017), 92.

30 Mitchell Dean, *Governmentality: Power and Rule in Modern Society* (2nd edn, Sage 2010), 56.

Bibliography

Afreen S and Abraham BP, 'Bioprospecting: Promoting and Regulating Access to Genetic Resources and Benefit Sharing' (2009) 36 *Decision* 121.

Anton D, 'Treaty Congestion in International Environmental Law' in Techera EJ (ed) *Routledge Handbook of International Environmental Law* (Routledge 2012).

Anuradha RV, 'In Search of Knowledge and Resources: Who Sows? Who Reaps?' (1997) 6 *Review of European Community and International Environmental Law* 263.

Ayal A, Hareuveny R and Perez O, 'Science, Politics and Transnational Regulation: Regulatory Scientific Institutions and the Dilemmas of Hybrid Authority' (2013) 2 *TEL* 45.

Bacchi C, 'Why Study Problematizations? Making Politics Visible' (2012) 2 *Open Journal of Political Science* 1.

Barbier EP, Burgess JC and Dean TJ, 'How to Pay for Saving Biodiversity: Can Private Sector Involvement in a Global Agreement Help to Conserve Global Biodiversity?' (2018) 360 *Science* 486.

Barry J, *Environment and Social Theory* (2nd edn, Routledge 2007).

Barton JH, 'Biodiversity at Rio' (1992) 42 *Bioscience* 773.

Berthoud G, 'Market' in Sachs W (ed) *The Development Dictionary: A Guide to Knowledge as Power* (Zed Books 1991).

Biermann F, Kanie N and Kim RE, 'Global Governance by Goal-Setting: The Novel Approach of the UN Sustainable Development Goals' (2017) 26–7 *Current Opinion in Environmental Sustainability* 26.

Bilderbeek S (ed), *Biodiversity and International Law: The Effectiveness of International Environmental Law* (IOS Press 1992).

Birch K and Tyfield D, 'Theorizing the Bioeconomy: Biovalue, Biocapital, Bioeconomics or ... What?' (2012) 38 *Science, Technology, & Human Values* 299.

Birnie P, Boyle AE and Redgwell C, *International Law and the Environment* (3rd edn, Oxford University Press 2009).

Bodansky D, *The Art and Craft of International Environmental Law* (Harvard University Press 2010).

Bosselman K, 'Poverty Alleviation and Environmental Sustainability through Improved Regimes of Technology Transfer' (2006) 2 *Law, Environment and Development Journal* 19.

Boulding KE, 'The Economics of the Coming Spaceship Earth' in Jarrety H (ed) *Environmental Quality in a Growing Economy* (The Johns Hopkins University Press 1966).

Bowman M, Davies P and Redgwell C, *Lyster's International Wildlife Law* (2nd edn, Cambridge University Press 2010).

108 Bibliography

Boyle AE, 'The Rio Convention on Biological Diversity' in Redgwell C and Bowman M (eds) *International Law and the Conservation of Biological Diversity* (Kluwer Law International 1995).

Brooks TM, Lamoreux JF and Soberón J, 'IPBES ≠ IPCC' (2014) 29 *Trends in Ecology & Evolution* 543.

Brown Weiss E, 'International Environmental Law: Contemporary Issues and the Emergence of a New World Order' (1993) 81 *Geo LJ* 675.

Bystrom M, Einarsson P and Nycander GA, *Fair and Equitable: Sharing the Benefits from Use of Genetic Resources and Traditional Knowledge* (Swedish Scientific Council on Biological Diversity 1999).

Coe M, 'African Wildlife Resources' in Soule ME and Wilcox BA (eds) *Conservation Biology: An Evolutionary-Ecological Perspective* (Sinauer Associates 1980).

Coetzee B, Gaston K and Chown S, 'Local Scale Comparisons of Biodiversity as a Test for Global Protected Area Ecological Performance: A Meta-Analysis' (2014) 9 *PloS one* e105824.

Coughlin MDJ, 'Using the Merck-INBio Agreement to Clarify the Convention on Biological Diversity' (1993) 31 *Colum J Transnat'l L* 337.

Deacon R, 'Theory as Practice: Foucault's Concept of Problematization' (2000) 118 *Telos* 127.

Dean M, *Governmentality: Power and Rule in Modern Society* (2nd edn, Sage 2010).

Dempsey J, *Enterprising Nature: Economics, Markets, and Finance in Global Biodiversity Politics* (Wiley Blackwell 2016).

Depledge J, 'The Opposite of Learning: Ossification in the Climate Change Regime' (2006) 6 *Global Environmental Politics* 1.

Dhar B, 'The Convention on Biological Diversity and the TRIPS Agreement: Compatibility or Conflict?' in Bellman C, Dutfield G and Melendez-Ortiz R (eds) *Trading in Knowledge: Development Perspectives on TRIP, Trade and Sustainability* (Earthscan 2003).

Díaz S, Demissew S, Carabias J, Joly C, Lonsdale M, Ash N, Larigauderie A, Adhikari J, Arico S, Báldi A, Bartuska A, Baste I, Bilgin A, Brondizio E, Chan KMA, Figueroa VE, Duraiappah A, Fischer M, Hill R, Koetz T, Leadley P, Lyver P, Mace GM, Martin-Lopez B, Okumura M, Pacheco D, Pascual U, Pérez ES, Reyers B, Roth E, Saito O, Scholes RJ, Sharma N, Tallis H, Thaman R, Watson R, Yahara T, Hamid ZA, Akosim C, Al-Hafedh Y, Allahverdiyev R, Amankwah E, Asah ST, Asfaw Z, Bartus G, Brooks LA, Caillaux J, Dalle G, Darnaedi D, Driver A, Erpul G, Escobar-Eyzaguirre Y, Failler P, Fouda, Y, Fu B, Gundimeda H, Hashimoto S, Homer F, Lavorel S, Lichtenstein G, Mala WA, Mandivenyi W, Matczak P, Mbivzo C, Mehrdadi M, Metzger JP, Mikissa JB, Moller H, Mooney HA, Mumby P, Nagendra H, Nesshover C, Oteng-Yeboah Y, Pataki G, Roué M, Rubis J, Schultz M, Smith P, Sumaila R, Takeuchi K, Thomas S, Verma M, Yeo-Chang Y and Zlatanova D, 'The IPBES Conceptual Framework: Connecting Nature and People' (2015) 14 *Current Opinion in Environmental Sustainability* 1.

Dinerstein E, Olson D, Joshi A, Vynne C, Burgess ND, Wikramanayake E, Hahn N, Palminteri S, Hedao P, Noss R, Hansen M, Locke H, Ellis EC, Jones B, Barber CV, Hayes R, Kormos C, Martin V, Crist E, Sechrest W, Price L, Baillie JEM, Weeden D, Suckling K, Davis C, Sizer N, Moore R, Thau D, Birch T, Potapov P, Turubanova S, Tyukavina A, de Souza N, Pintea L, Brito JC, Llewellyn OA, Miller AG, Patzelt A, Ghazanfar SA, Timberlake J, Klöser H, Shennan-Farpón Y, Kindt R, Lillesø JPB, van Breugel P, Graudal L, Voge M, Al-Shammari KF and Saleem M, 'An Ecoregion-Based Approach to Protecting Half the Terrestrial Realm' (2017) 67 *BioScience* 534.

Douzinas C and Geary A, *Critical Jurisprudence: The Political Philosophy of Justice* (Hart Publishing 2005).

Driesen DM, 'Thirty Years of International Environmental Law: A Retrospective and Plea for Reinvigoration' (2003) 30 *Syracuse J Int'l L & Com* 353.

Duvic-Paoli L-A, 'The Intergovernmental Science-Policy Platform for Biodiversity and Ecosystem Services or the Framing of Scientific Knowledge within the Law of Sustainable Development' (2017) 19 *ICLR* 231.

Editorial, 'Wanted: An IPCC for Biodiversity' (2010) 465 *Nature* 525.

Ehrenfeld D, *Biological Conservation* (Holt, Rinehart and Winston, Inc. 1970).

Ehrenfeld D, 'Why Put a Value on Biodiversity?' in Wilson EO (ed) *Biodiversity* (National Academy Press 1988).

Ehrlich P, 'The Strategy of Conservation 1980–2000' in Soule ME and Wilcox BA (eds) *Conservation Biology: An Evolutionary - Ecological Perspective* (Sinauer Associates 1980).

Ehrlich P, 'The Loss of Diversity: Causes and Consequences' in Wilson EO (ed) *Biodiversity* (National Academy Press 1988).

Ehrlich PR and Ehrlich AH, *Extinction: The Causes and Consequences of the Disappearance of Species* (Gollancz 1981).

Ehrlich PR, Ehrlich AH and Holdren JP, *Ecoscience: Population, Resources, Environment* (W.H. Freeman and Co 1972).

Eisner T, 'Prospecting for Nature's Chemical Riches' (1990) 6 *Issues in Science and Technology* 31.

Eisner T, 'Chemical Prospecting: A Proposal for Action' in Bormann FH and Kellert SR (eds) *Ecology, Economics, Ethics: The Broken Circle* (Yale University Press 1991).

Eisner T, 'Chemical Prospecting: A Global Imperative' (1994) 138 *Proceedings of the American Philosophical Society* 385.

Eisner T and Beiring EA, 'Biotic Exploration Fund: Protecting Biodiversity through Chemical Prospecting' (1994) 44 *Bioscience* 95.

Esteva G, 'Development' in Sachs W (ed) *The Development Dictionary: A Guide to Knowledge as Power* (2nd edn, Zed Books 2010).

Farnham TJ, *Saving Nature's Legacy: Origins of the Idea of Biological Diversity* (Yale University Press 2007).

Flitner M, 'Biodiversity: Of Local Commons and Global Commodities' in Goldman M (ed) *Privatizing Nature: Political Struggles for the Global Commons* (Pluto Press 1998).

Flynn T, 'Foucault's Mapping of History' in Gutting G (ed) *The Cambridge Companion to Foucault* (2nd edn, Cambridge University Press 2003).

Foucault M, 'The Concern for Truth' in Kritzman LD (ed) *Michel Foucault Politics, Philosophy, Culture: Interviews and Other Writings 1977–1984* (Routledge 1988).

Foucault M, 'Nietzsche, Genealogy, History' in Rabinow P (ed) *The Foucault Reader: An Introduction to Foucault's Thought* (Penguin 1991).

Foucault M, 'On the Genealogy of Ethics: An Overview of a Work in Progress' in Rabinow P (ed) *The Foucault Reader: An Introduction to Foucault's Thought* (Penguin 1991).

Foucault M, 'Questions of Method' in Burchell G, Gordon C and Miller P (eds) *The Foucault Effect: Studies in Governmentality* (University of Chicago Press 1991).

Foucault M, *The Use of Pleasure: The History of Sexuality Volume 2* (Penguin 1992 [1984]).

Foucault M, *The Will to Knowledge: The History of Sexuality Volume 1* (Penguin 1998 [1976]).

Foucault M, 'Nietzsche, Genealogy, History' in Faubion JD (ed) *Aesthetics, Method and Espistemology: Essential Works of Foucault 1954–1984 Volume 2* (Penguin 2000).

110   Bibliography

Foucault M, 'Polemics, Politics and Problematizations' in Rabinow P (ed) *Ethics: Subjectivity and Truth* (Penguin 2000).

Foucault M, *Fearless Speech* (Semiotext(e) 2001).

Foucault M, 'What is Called "Punishing"?' in Faubion JD (ed) *Power: Essential Works of Focault 1954–1984 Volume Three* (Penguin 2002).

Francioni F, 'Foreword' in Morgera E, Tsioumani E and Buck M (eds) *Unraveling the Nagoya Protocol: A Commentary on the Nagoya Protocol on Access and Benefit-Sharing to the Convention on Biological Diversity* (Brill 2015).

Furedi F, *Population and Development: A Critical Introduction* (Polity Press 1997).

Gamez R, 'The Link between Biodiversity and Sustainable Development: Lessons from INBio's Bioprospecting Programme in Costa Rica' in McManis CR (ed) *Biodiversity and the Law: Intellectual Property, Biotechnology & Traditional Knowledge* (Earthscan 2007).

Gamez R, Piva A, Sittenfield A, Leon E, Jimenez J and Mirabelli G, 'Costa Rica's Conservation Program and National Biodiversity Institute (INBio)' in Reid WV, Laird SA, Meyer CA, Gamez R, Sittenfield A, Janzen DH, Gollin MA and Juma C (eds) *Biodiversity Prospecting: Using Genetic Resources for Sustainable Development* (World Resources Institute (WRI) 1993).

Gillespie A, *The Illusion of Progress: Unsustainable Development in International Law and Policy* (Earthscan 2001).

Glowka L, 'Emerging Legislative Approaches to Implement Article 15 of the Convention on Biological Diversity' (1997) 6 *Review of European Community and International Environmental Law* 249.

Goeschl T, Gatti R, Groom B and Swanson T, 'Incentivizing Ecological Destruction? The Global Joint Regulation of the Conservation and Use of Genetic Resources' (2005) 38 *Ind L Rev* 619.

Golder B, 'Contemporary Legal Genealogies' in Desautels-Stein J and Tomlins C (eds) *Searching for Contemporary Legal Thought* (Cambridge University Press 2017).

Goldman M, 'Eco-governmentality and Other Transnational Practices of a "Green" World Bank' in Peet R and Watts M (eds) *Liberation Ecologies: Environment, Development, Social Movements* (2nd edn, Routledge 2004).

Goldman M (ed), *Privatizing Nature: Political Struggles for the Global Commons* (Transnational Institute Series, Pluto Press 1998).

Goldstein J (ed), *Foucault and the Writing of History* (Blackwell 1994).

Görg C, Neßhöver C and Paulsch A, 'A New Link between Biodiversity Science and Policy' (2010) 19 *GAIA - Ecological Perspectives for Science and Society* 183.

Guha R and Martinez-Alier J, *Varieties of Environmentalism: Essays North and South* (Earthscan 1997).

Gunningham N, 'Environmental Law, Regulation, and Governance: Shifting Architectures' (2009) 21 *JEL* 179.

Harvey D, *Justice, Nature and the Geography of Difference* (Blackwell Publishing 1996).

Helmreich S, 'Blue-Green Capital, Biotechnological Circulation and an Oceanic Imaginary: A Critique of Biopolitical Economy' (2007) 2 *Biosocieties* 287.

IUCN, UNEP and WWF, *World Conservation Strategy: Living Resource Conservation for Sustainable Development* (1980).

Jaeckel A, 'Intellectual Property Rights and the Conservation of Plant Biodiversity as a Common Concern of Humankind' (2013) 2 *TEL* 167.

Janzen DH, 'Tropical Ecological and Biocultural Restoration' (1988) 239 *Science* 243.

Janzen DH, 'How to Save Tropical Biodiversity: The National Biodiversity Institute of Costa Rica' (1991) 37 *American Entomologist* 159.

Koester V, 'The Five Global Biodiversity-Related Conventions: A Stocktaking' (2002) 11 *Review of European Community and International Environmental Law* 96.

Koopman C, *Genealogy as Critique: Foucault and the Problems of Modernity* (Indiana University Press 2013).

Kotsakis A, 'Change and Subjectivity in International Environmental Law: The Micro-Politics of the Transformation of Biodiversity into Genetic Gold' (2014) 3 *TEL* 127.

Laird SA (ed), *Biodiversity and Traditional Knowledge: Equitable Partnerships in Practice* (People and Plants Conservation Series, Earthscan 2002).

Laird SA and Wynberg R, *Bioscience at a Crossroads: Implementing the Nagoya Protocol on Access and Benefit Sharing in a Time of Scientific, Technological and Industry Change* (Secretariat of the Convention on Biological Diversity 2012).

Larigauderie A and Mooney HA, 'The Intergovernmental Science-Policy Platform on Biodiversity and Ecosystem Services: Moving a Step Closer to an IPCC-like Mechanism for Biodiversity' (2010) 2 *Current Opinion in Environmental Sustainability* 9.

Lautenschlager RA, 'Biodiversity is Dead' (1997) 25 *Wildlife Society Bulletin* 679.

Le Prestre PG (ed), *Governing Global Biodiversity: The Evolution and Implementation of the Convention on Biological Diversity* (Routledge 2002).

Le Prestre PG, 'Introduction: The Emergence of Global Biodiversity Governance' in Le Prestre PG (ed) *Governing Global Biodiversity: The Evolution and Implementation of the Convention on Biological Diversity* (Routledge 2002).

Lewin R, 'Costa Rican Biodiversity' (1988) 242 *Science* 1637.

Lyster S, *International Wildlife Law: An Analysis of International Treaties Concerned with the Conservation of Wildlife* (Grotius 1985).

Martínez Alier J, *The Environmentalism of the Poor: A Study of Ecological Conflicts and Valuation* (Edward Elgar Publishing 2002).

Martinez SI and Biber-Klemm S, 'Scientists – Take Action for Access to Biodiversity' (2010) 2 *Current Opinion in Environmental Sustainability* 27.

McAfee K, 'Selling Nature to Save it? Biodiversity and Green Developmentalism' (1999) 17 *Environment and Planning D: Society and Space* 133.

McAfee K, 'Neoliberalism on the Molecular Scale: Economic and Genetic Reductionism in Biotechnology Battles' (2003) 34 *Geoforum* 203.

McConnell F, *The Biodiversity Convention: A Negotiating History* (Kluwer Law International 1996).

McEldowney J and McEldowney S, 'Science and Environmental Law: Collaboration across the Double Helix' (2011) 13 *Environmental Law Review* 169.

McNeely JA, Miller KR, Reid WV, Mittermeier RA and Werner TB, *Conserving the World's Biological Diversity* (IUCN 1990).

Miller JS, 'Impact of the Convention on Biological Diversity: The Lessons from Ten Years of Experience with Models of Equitable Sharing of Benefits' in McManis CR (ed) *Biodiversity and the Law: Intellectual Property, Biotechnology and Traditional Knowledge* (Earthscan 2007).

Moore NW, 'Experience with Pesticides and the Theory of Conservation' (1969) 1 *Biological Conservation* 201.

Moore NW and Tatton JOG, 'Organochlorine Insecticide Residues in the Eggs of Sea Birds' (1965) 207 *Nature* 42.

112   Bibliography

Myers N, *The Sinking Ark: A New Look at the Problem of Disappearing Species* (Pergamon 1979).

Najam A, 'Developing Countries and Global Environmental Governance: From Contestation to Participation to Engagement' (2005) 5 *International Environmental Agreements* 303.

Nayar RJ and Ong DM, 'Developing Countries, "Development" and the Conservation of Biological Diversity' in Redgwell C and Bowman M (eds) *International Law and the Conservation of Biological Diversity* (Kluwer Law International 1995).

Norse EA, 'A River that Flows to the Sea: The Marine Biological Diversity Movement' (1996) 9 *Oceanography* 5.

Norse EA and McManus RE, 'Ecology and Living Resources: Biological Diversity' (1980) *Environmental Quality 1980: The Eleventh Annual Report of the Council on Environmental Quality*.

Ong DM, 'International Environmental Law Governing Threats to Biodiversity' in Fitzmaurice M, Ong DM and Merkouris P (eds) *Research Handbook on International Environmental Law* (Edward Elgar 2010).

Palmer G, 'New Ways to Make International Environmental Law' (1992) 86 *American Journal of International Law* 259.

Pascual U, Balvanera P, Díaz S, Pataki G, Roth E, Stenseke M, Watson RT, Başak Dessane E, Islar M, Kelemen E, Maris V, Quaas M, Subramanian SM, Wittmer H, Adlan A, Ahn S, Al-Hafedh Y, Amankwah E, Asah ST, Berry P, Bilgin A, Breslow SJ, Bullock C, Cáceres D, Daly-Hassen Y, Figueroa E, Golden CD, Gómez-Baggethun Y, González-Jiménez Y, Houdet J, Keune H, Kumar R, Ma K, May PH, Mead A, O'Farrell P, Pandit R, Pengue W, Pichis-Madruga Y, Popa F, Preston S, Pacheco-Balanza Y, Saarikoski H, Strassburg BB, van den Belt M, Verma M, Wickson F and Yagi N, 'Valuing Nature's Contributions to People: The TPBES Approach' (2017) 26–27 *Current Opinion in Environmental Sustainability* 7.

Perez O, 'The Hybrid Legal-Scientific Dynamic of Transnational Scientific Institutions' (2015) 26 *EJIL* 391.

Peterson GD, Harmáková ZV, Meacham M, Queiroz C, Jiménez-Aceituno Y, Kuiper JJ, Malmborg K, Sitas N and Bennett EM, 'Welcoming Different Perspectives in IPBES: "Nature's Contributions to People" and "Ecosystem Services"' (2018) 23 *Ecology and Society* 39.

Philippopoulos-Mihalopoulos A, 'Looking for the Space between Law and Ecology' in Philippopoulos-Mihalopoulos A (ed) *Law and Ecology: New Environmental Legal Foundations* (Routledge 2011).

Philippopoulos-Mihalopoulos A, '"…The Sound of Breaking String": Critical Environmental Law and Ontological Vulnerability' (2011) 2 *Journal of Human Rights and the Environment* 5.

Rajamani L, 'From Stockholm to Johannesburg: The Anatomy of Dissonance in the International Environmental Dialogue' (2003) 12 *Review of European Community and International Environmental Law* 23.

Reaka-Kudla ML, Wilson DE and Wilson EO (eds), *Biodiversity II: Understanding and Protecting Our Biological Resources* (Joseph Henry Press 1996).

Reid WV, Laird SA, Meyer CA, Gamez R, Sittenfield A, Janzen DH, Gollin MA and Juma C, *Biodiversity Prospecting: Using Genetic Resources for Sustainable Development* (World Resources Institute 1993).

Bibliography 113

Rubino MC, 'Biodiversity Finance' (2000) 76 *International Affairs* 223.

Sand PH, 'Sovereignty Bounded: Public Trusteeship for Common Pool Resources?' (2004) 4 *Global Environmental Politics* 47.

Sand PH, 'The Evolution of International Environmental Law' in Bodansky D, Brunnée J and Hey E (eds) *The Oxford Handbook of International Environmental Law* (OUP 2007).

Schellenberger M and Nordhaus T, *Break Through: From the Death of Environmentalism to the Politics of Possibility* (Houghton Mifflin Co. 2007).

Shine C and Kohona PTB, 'The Convention on Biological Diversity: Bridging the Gap between Conservation and Development' (1992) 1 *Review of European Community and International Environmental Law* 278.

Shiva V, *Monocultures of the Mind: Perspectives on Biodiversity and Biotechnology* (Zed Books 1993).

Soule ME, 'What is Conservation Biology?' (1985) 35 *Bioscience* 727.

Soule ME, 'Conservation and the "Real World"' in Soule ME (ed) *Conservation Biology: The Science of Scarcity and Diversity* (Sinauer 1986).

Soule ME, 'Tactics for a Constant Crisis' (1991) 253 *Science* 744.

Soule ME, 'The Social Seige of Nature' in Soule ME and Lease G (eds) *Reinventing Nature? Responses to Postmodern Deconstruction* (Island Press 1995).

Soule ME and Wilcox BA (eds), *Conservation Biology: An Evolutionary – Ecological Perspective* (Sinauer 1980).

Swanson T, 'The Reliance of Northern Economies on Southern Biodiversity: Biodiversity as Information' (1996) 17 *Ecological Economics* 1.

Swanson T, 'Why is There a Biodiversity Convention? The International Interest in Centralized Development Planning' (1999) 75 *International Affairs* 307.

Takacs D, *The Idea of Biodiversity: Philosophies of Paradise* (Johns Hopkins University Press 1996).

Tangley L, 'Cataloging Costa Rica's Diversity' (1990) 40 *BioScience* 633.

Tarlock AD, 'Who Owns Science?' (2002) 10 *Penn State Environmental Law Review* 135.

ten Kate K, 'Science and the Convention on Biological Diversity' (2002) 295 *Science* 2371.

ten Kate K and Laird SA, *The Commercial Use of Biodiversity* (Earthscan 1999).

ten Kate K and Laird SA, 'Biodiversity and Business: Coming to Terms with the "Grand Bargain"' (2000) 76 *International Affairs* 241.

Tinker C, 'A "New Breed" of Treaty: The United Nations Convention on Biological Diversity' (1995) 13 *Pace Envtl L Rev* 191.

Tully S, 'The Bonn Guidelines on Access to Genetic Resources and Benefit Sharing' (2003) 12 *Review of European Community and International Environmental Law* 84.

Tushnet M, 'Critical Legal Theory (without Modifiers) in the United States' (2005) 13 *The Journal of Political Philosophy* 99.

Tushnet M, 'Some Current Controversies in Critical Legal Studies' (2011) 12 *German Law Journal* 290.

Vadrot A, *The Politics of Knowledge and Global Biodiversity* (Routledge 2014).

Veyne P, 'Foucault Revolutionizes History' in Davidson AI (ed) *Foucault and His Interlocutors* (University of Chicago Press 1997).

Vogel JH, 'From the "Tragedy of the Commons" to the "Tragedy of the Commonplace": Analysis and Synthesis through the Lens of Economic Theory' in McManis CR (ed) *Biodiversity and the Law: Intellectual Property, Biotechnology & Traditional Knowledge* (Earthscan 2007).

Watts M, 'Development and Governmentality' (2003) 24 *Singapore Journal of Tropical Geography* 6.

Wilson EO (ed), *BioDiversity* (National Academy Press 1988).

Zebich-Knos M, 'Preserving Biodiversity in Costa Rica: The Case of the Merck-INBio Agreement' (1997) 6 *The Journal of Environment & Development* 180.

Index

ABS Clearing House 84
access and benefit sharing (ABS): for academic and applied research 90–91; access permits 84; agricultural practices and 87; basic principle of 83–84; biodiversity convention and 1–2, 42, 78, 80–84, 86, 93n9; biodiversity loss and 42; bioprospecting and 81, 89–90; Bonn guidelines and 81, 84; capacity-building and 84; central benefit-sharing mechanisms 85–86; conservation funding and 89–90; fair and equitable 2–3, 83–85, 94n46; genetic resources and 78–80, 82–87; informed consent for 83; local/indigenous community involvement in 82–83; market regulation and 79; Nagoya Protocol and 1–3, 78, 80–83, 85–87, 89–92; North-South balance and x, 42; public/private arrangements 92; sustainable development and 72
African Model Law 79
agriculture: access and benefit sharing (ABS) 87; bioprospecting as 67; competition with nature reserves 25; FAO Treaty and 85; genetic diversity in 28; germplasm resources and 26; threat to biological diversity 27–28
Aichi Biodiversity Targets 2, 6–7, 96
Andean Pact, Decision 391 79, 93n10

Bible of Biodiversity 32–34, 52
biocultural restoration 68
biodiscovery 91
biodiversity: biotechnology and 51; commodification of 49, 92; as common heritage 55; conceptual interdependence in 33; defining 2; development and 53; economic value of 101; familiarity and 33; as genetic gold ix, x, 31, 53, 67, 71–73; as genetic resources 66–68, 97; governmental programmes and 98; historicization of 17; innovation and 33; internationalization of 50; as national resource 2, 99; overpopulation threats to 24–25, 28, 30, 34–35; as political technology 100; politics of ix, 50; popularization of 32, 34; problematization of 34–38, 42, 46–49, 52, 55, 98–99; productive use of 38; sustainable development and 30–31, 47, 49–50, 57, 62, 65, 67, 70; target setting in 96; terminological shift to 23, 32, 46; treaty violations and 99; as under-utilized resource 61–64, 68; wild 87–88, 90; *see also* biodiversity loss; biological diversity; genetic resources
biodiversity conservation: acquisition of nature reserves 25, 28, 96; active 25; cooperative efforts for 63–64; ecosystem approach 28; feedback loop in 66; funding for 73–74, 89–90; gene bank-zoo-botanical garden approach 28, 63; genetic gold and 73–74; geographical focus of 31; government policies for 64–65, 69; human interests and 25; instrumental value and 27, 31, 49; intellectual property rights and 92n3; intrinsic value and 27; market-based approaches to 64, 67; problematization and 24–27, 31, 38; regimes of practices and 23–24; *in situ* conservation 2, 31, 55, 63; species approach 28; strategic objectives of 25–26; valuable species protection 25
biodiversity convention (CBD): access and benefit sharing (ABS) 2–3, 42,

78, 80–84, 86, 93n9; bioprospecting regulation and 71; Bonn guidelines 80–81, 84, 92; common concern of humanity in 54; conservation goals 2–4, 91–92, 102; development of viii; funding arrangements in 48, 73, 77n76, 77n79; genetic gold and 18, 62, 70–73, 78–79; global biodiversity regime and x; global bioeconomy and 79; historical narrative and 98–99, 103; institutional structure of 4–5; international environmental law and 1; IPBES and 102; jurisdictional limitations of 3–4; lack of implementation mechanisms for 7–8; legal genealogy of ix, 11–14, 17, 57, 97–101, 103; living modified organisms (LMOs) 92n2; national implementation and 80; North–South balance and x, 3, 49–50, 56–57, 73, 80; permanent sovereignty over natural resources in 49, 54–55; persistence of 97, 100; as platform for solutions 100; regulation and 80; strategic planning and 7, 17, 22n107; sustainable development and 92; sustainable use and 2–3, 91; technology transfer and 51–52; treaty regime of 1–8, 11, 17, 103; valuation of biodiversity resources 63; *see also* Nagoya Protocol

biodiversity loss: benefits sharing and 42; bioprospecting benefits and 69; conservation biology and 31–32, 34; ecological truth of 8; economic growth and 48; Global South and 36; habitat destruction and 35–36; international law and 17–18, 54; lack of impact on 7, 97; legal focus on response to 8–11; overexploitation and 48, 50; population and 35–36, 48; problematization of 18, 31; treaty regime and 17

Biodiversity Prospecting (Reid et al.) 70

biodiversity reason x, 38, 65–66, 100

bioeconomy: access and benefit sharing (ABS) 91; biodiversity convention and 79; bioprospecting and 70, 91; Costa Rica and 69–70, 72; environmental outcomes of 89–90; genetic gold and 61, 72, 79, 84, 89–90, 97; global market for 61, 70; INBio and 69; North–South balance and 80; policy manuals for 70–71; public/private arrangements 92; under-utilization of biodiversity and 61

biological diversity: conservation biology and 29–34, 47; defining 2, 26; economic potential of 27; environmental discourse and 23–24; future value of 27, 29, 39n35; human impact on 27–29; material benefits of 27; planned practices for 25; popularization of 33; problematization and 38, 47; protection of the whole 25–26; sustainable use and 2; terminological shift to biodiversity 23, 32, 46; as wasted resource 31; *see also* biodiversity

biological heritage 28

bioprospecting: access and benefit sharing (ABS) 81, 89–90; as agriculture 67; benefits sharing and 81; bioeconomy and 70, 91; biotechnology industry and 69, 87–88; chemical ecology and 66; environmental policy and 89; feedback loop in 66; genetic gold and 68–70, 88; genetic resources and 70–71, 87, 91; INBio and 65–70; private partnerships in 66–68; regulation of 71, 81

biotechnology industry: bioprospecting and 69, 87–88; *ex situ* genetic material 88–89; genetic resources and ix, 3, 50–51, 80, 82, 87; intellectual property rights of 51–52; research and development 88–89; technology transfer and 51–52; use of derivates 82

Birnie, Patricia 54

Bonn guidelines 80–81, 84, 92

Boulding, Kenneth 30

Bowman, Michael 54

Boyle, Alan 56

Brundtland Report 44–47

Cancun Declaration (2002) 53, 71

Carson, Rachel 10, 31–32, 34

Cartagena Protocol 1, 78, 92n2

CBD *see* biodiversity convention (CBD)

chemical ecology 66

conservation: anti-economic attitudes 29–30; attitudes towards 24–25; biological heritage and 28; complex human problems and 24, 26; defining 2; failure to incorporate ecology and biology in 29–30; holistic/instrumental practices 25; human exploitation/utilization and 31; practices and 23; problematization of 24, 26, 28; *in situ* 2, 31, 55, 63; *see also* biodiversity conservation

Index 117

conservation biology: anti-economic attitudes 30–31, 57; biodiversity and 29–34, 38, 47; biodiversity loss and 31–32, 34; environmentalism and 34; on obstacles to effective conservation 29–30; politics and 37, 50; rainforest/ tropics focus of 32, 36

Conservation Biology (Ehrlich) 30–31, 36–37

Conserving the World's Biological Diversity (IUCN) 62

Consultative Group on International Agricultural Research (CGIAR) 85–86

Costa Rica 65–69, 72

Council on Environmental Quality (CEQ) 26–28, 42

custodial sovereignty 54

Daly, Herman 30

derivatives 3, 19n24, 81–82

ecological debt 48–49

ecosystem services 102, 105n28

Ehrenfeld, David 30

Ehrlich, Paul 30, 35–36, 48–49

Eisner, Thomas 66, 91

Eleventh Annual Report (CEQ) 26

environmentalism: anti-economic attitudes 30–31, 37, 57; biodiversity and 37; conservation biology and 34; conservation efforts and 69; sustainable development and 50

Environmental Perspective for the Year 2000 and beyond (WCED) 45, 47

FAO *see* Food and Agriculture Organization of the United Nations (FAO)

FAO Treaty 85–86

feedback loop 66

Food and Agriculture Organization of the United Nations (FAO) 70, 85–86

Foucault, Michel: fetishization of 14, 16–17; genealogical approach 11–14, 16–17; on genealogy versus history of ideas 22n90; on practices 13; on problematization 11–12, 21n76; on rules of conduct 14

Francioni, Francesco 54

Gamez, Rodrigo 66–67

genealogy: contingency and 15–16; critical inquiry and 11; Foucault and 11–14,

16–17; governmental thought and 18; historicization and 11–12, 14–15; history and 14; practices and 12–13; precedent and 15; problematization and 11–14, 21n76; programmes of conduct and 13; thought and 14; *see also* legal genealogy

genetic diversity 26, 28, 35, 43

genetic gold: access and benefit sharing (ABS) 78; biodiversity as ix, x, 31, 53, 67, 71–73; biodiversity convention and 18, 62, 70–73, 78–79; bioeconomy and 61, 70, 72, 79, 84, 87, 89–90; bioprospecting and 68–70, 88; conservation funding and 73–74; end of 91–92; individual/community empowerment and 72, 77n74; international environmental law and 61–62, 78; Nagoya Protocol and 5–6; pharmaceutical research trends and 88; as programme of conduct 13; regulation of 78–92; sustainable development and 70–71, 73–74; under-utilization of biodiversity and 61

genetic resources: access and benefit sharing (ABS) 79–80, 82–87; application of 82; biodiversity as 66–68, 97; biodiversity convention and 79, 82; bioeconomy and 89; bioprospecting and 70–71, 87, 91; biotechnology industry and 3, 50–51, 80, 82, 87; certification systems 84; commercialization of 82, 88; defining 82; derivatives 3, 19n24; development and 71–72; drug discovery and 76n38; economic value of 62–74, 87, 101; *ex situ* material 88–89, 95n73; local/ indigenous communities and 82–83; market practices and 87–88, 90–91; market regulation and 79; national sovereignty and 3, 79; plant 85–86; post-colonialism and 72; preparatory tasks and 88–89; regulation of 79, 81–89; under-utilization of 61–62, 68; utilization of 3, 82, 88; wild biodiversity 87–88; *see also* biodiversity conservation

Global Biodiversity Outlook 7

Global Biodiversity Strategy 70, 73

Global Environment Facility 73

Global North: benefits sharing and x, 42; biodiversity loss narrative and 48; biodiversity resources and 80; development assistance 90; ecological debt and 48–49; funding of

118 Index

Southern conservation 43, 57; genetic resources and 50, 71; Global South exchange 42, 47–48, 56, 73, 80, 92; historical responsibilities of 37, 48; international environmental law and 80; overexploitation of resources and 48, 50; on Southern underdevelopment 61; technology transfer and 51–52

Global South: benefits sharing and x, 42, 66; biodiversity loss narrative and 48; biodiversity resources ix, 48–49, 62, 87; funding of conservation efforts 43, 50; genetic gold and 91; Global North exchange 42, 47–48, 73, 80, 90, 92; habitat destruction in 36; historical responsibilities of 37, 48; international environmental fora and 58n34; national regulatory capacity and 81; perceived overpopulation of 37, 48, 50; permanent sovereignty over natural resources in 43, 49; political economy and 36, 50–51; problematization of biodiversity and 36–37; sustainable development and 47–50, 67–68; technology transfer and 51–52; under-utilization of biodiversity and 61–62; see also Like-Minded Group of Mega Diverse Countries (LLMC)

Golder, Ben 11–12, 15

Group of 77 (G77) 92n4

habitat destruction 35–36

human population: biodiversity loss and 48; habitat destruction by 35–36; impact of 24–25, 28, 30, 34–37; overpopulation fears 37, 41n108, 48; problematization of 35–37

INBio: biodiversity reason and 65–66; bioprospecting and 65–70, 87; Costa Rican bioeconomy and 69, 73; development and 53

INBio-Merck partnership 68–70, 87

indigenous communities 3, 63, 82–83, 85

intellectual property rights 51–52, 92n3

Intergovernmental Science–Policy Platform on Biodiversity and Ecosystem Services (IPBES) 101–102, 104n18, 105n28

International Agricultural Research Centres (IARCs) 85

International Cooperative Biodiversity Groups 76n38

international environmental law: *a priori* environmental problems and 9–11; benefits sharing and 42; biodiversity convention and 1–8; biodiversity loss and 54; biodiversity protection and 45–48; biotechnology and 51–52; Brundtland Report and 44–47; Cancun Declaration (2002) 53; conservation treaties 50; ethic of equity 53; genetic gold and 61–62, 78; global political economy and 45; historical legitimacy in 9–11, 98–99; hope for progress in 5; within international law 4–5, 80; interventionism and 49; IUCN and 43–44, 55–56; national sovereignty and 54–55; North–South balance and 56–57, 80; overpopulation and 48; problematization and 14, 52, 55–57; public trusteeship model 54–55; technology transfer and 51–52; teleology of 8–11, 15; UNEP and 44–47; WCED and 45; Western Hemisphere Convention 4; World Conservation Strategy (WCS) 42–43; *see also* biodiversity convention (CBD)

international law: biodiversity conservation and 45–48, 55–57; environmental law within 4–5, 80; legal genealogy and 15, 17–18; problematization of 55–57; species convention and 44; target setting in 13; universal principles and 100; US conservation obligations in 28; Westphalian model of 54

International Union for the Conservation of Nature (IUCN) 43–44, 55–56, 70

International Year of Biodiversity 5

IPBES *see* Intergovernmental Science–Policy Platform on Biodiversity and Ecosystem Services (IPBES)

IUCN *see* International Union for the Conservation of Nature (IUCN)

Janzen, Daniel 65–66

Klemm, Cyrile de 43

Koopman, Colin 13, 16

Lautenschlager, R. A. 96

legal genealogy: biodiversity convention and 11–14, 17, 57, 97–101, 103; contingency and 14–16, 98; defining 11; Foucaultianism and 14, 16–17;

governmental thought and 18; historicization and 14–15, 98; inquiry and 11; masking of power and 14, 16; methodology of 11, 14, 21n72; practices and 12–14; problematization and 11–14; programmes of conduct and 13; *see also* genealogy
Like-Minded Group of Mega Diverse Countries (LLMC) 52–53, 57, 61
Lovejoy, Thomas 65
Lyster, Simon 5

McConnell, Fiona 46
McManus, Roger 26, 42
Merck 66–67, 87; *see also* INBio-Merck partnership
Millennium Development Goals (MDGs) 7
Monbiot, George 6
Monks Wood experimentation station 24
Moore, Norman 24–26, 28, 30–31, 34

Nagoya Conference 5–6
Nagoya–Kuala Lumpur Supplementary Protocol on Liability and Redress 1
Nagoya Protocol: access and benefit sharing (ABS) 1–3, 78, 80–83, 85–87, 89–92; biotechnology use of derivates 82; genetic gold response 5–6; legal definitions in 82; legal effect of 86–87; market practices and 90, 92, 100; as quasi-soft law 99; strategic planning and 7
National Biodiversity Conservation and Sustainable Use Strategy 68
National Biodiversity Institute (INBio) *see* INBio
National Biodiversity Strategy and Action Plans 7
National Cancer Institute 76n38
National Forum on BioDiversity (1986) 32–34
National Research Council 32
Nature Conservancy 24
nature conservation 23–25, 46; *see also* biodiversity conservation; conservation
NBSAPs (National Biodiversity Strategies and Action Plans) 4
New International Economic Order (NIEO) 49, 53
NIEO *see* New International Economic Order (NIEO)
Norse, Elliot ix, 26, 42

overconsumption 48

Pasça Palmer, Cristiana 101
pesticides 24–25
plant genetic resources 85–86
practices 12–13, 18, 25
problematization: attitudes towards conservation and 24; of biodiversity 34–38, 42, 46–49, 52, 55, 98–99; conservation practices and 38; genealogy and 11–14; international environmental law and 14, 52, 55–57; practices and 12–13; reorientation of genealogy and 21n76; thought and 14, 22n90
programmes 13, 17–18, 25–26
public trusteeship model 54–55

rainforest 9, 32, 36, 49
Redgwell, Catherine 54
Report of the World Commission on Environment and Development (Brundtland Report) *see* Brundtland Report
Rio Summit *see* UN Conference on Environment and Development (UNCED)

Shaman Pharmaceuticals 88
Silent Spring (Carson) 32
Smithsonian Institute 32, 34
Soule, Michael 30–31
state sovereignty: biodiversity convention and 79; genetic resources and 3, 79; international environmental law and 54–55; of natural resources 43, 49, 54–55; problematization of 55; public trusteeship model 54–55
sustainable development: biodiversity and 30–31, 47, 49–50, 57, 62, 67, 70; biodiversity convention and 92; environmentalism and 50; genetic gold and 70–71, 73–74; Global South and 47–50, 67–68; individual/community empowerment and 72
sustainable use 2–3, 91, 93n26
Swanson, Timothy 56
synthetic biology 88, 91

technology transfer 51–52
traditional knowledge 62, 82–83, 85
treaty regimes: access and benefit sharing (ABS) 81; biodiversity convention

120 Index

as 1–5, 8, 11, 17, 103; institutional practices and 4

UNCLOS *see* UN Convention on the Law of the Sea (UNCLOS)
UN Conference on Environment and Development (UNCED) 47, 55
UN Conference on the Human Environment 98
UN Convention on Biological Diversity (CBD) *see* biodiversity convention (CBD)
UN Convention on the Law of the Sea (UNCLOS) 44
UN Environment Programme (UNEP) 44–47, 70, 104n19
UNESCO 70
UN General Assembly (UNGA) 45
United Nations Decade on Biodiversity 6
US environmental law 26–27

WCED *see* World Commission on Environment and Development (WCED)
Western Hemisphere Convention 4
wild biodiversity 87–88, 90
wildlife resources 36–37
Wilson, Edward 65, 74
World Bank: biodiversity conservation and 64; management of biodiversity as resource 62–64, 67–68, 70, 72–73
World Commission on Environment and Development (WCED) 45
World Conservation Strategy (WCS) 28, 42–44
World Resources Institute (WRI) 70
World Summit of Sustainable Development 7
World Trade Organization (WTO) 51–52